SLEEPING
with
DIONYSUS

SLEEPING
with
DIONYSUS

WOMEN, ECSTASY
AND ADDICTION

Kay Marie Porterfield

The Crossing Press, Freedom, CA 95019

Cover painting by Sheryl McCartney
Cover design by Sheryl Karas

Printed in the U.S.A.

Library of Congress Cataloging-in-Publication Data

Sleeping with Dionysus : women, ecstacy, and addiction / (compiled)
by Kay Marie Porterfield.
     p.   cm.
  ISBN 0-89594-653-X. — ISBN 0-89594-652-1 (pbk.)
   1. Women—United States—Drug use—Literary collections.
2. Substance abuse—United States—Literary collections.
3. Women—United States—Alcohol use—Literary collections.
4. Women—United States—Sexual behavior—Literary collections.
5. American literature—Women authors. 6. American literature—
20th century.
I. Porterfield, Kay Marie.
PS509.W6S54   1994
810.8' 0355—dc20   93-23620
                                           CIP

Table of Contents

IV. Recovery: Out of the Maze 117

V. Reclaiming the Goddess Within 169

About the Authors 203

Acknowledgments

Annie Dawid: "Blacking Out" originally appeared in *Rigorous*, Fall 1992. Reprinted by permission of the author.

Catherine Gammon: "Trespass" originally appeared in *The Iowa Review:* Winter, 1988, and as part of *Isabel Out of the Rain:* Mercury House, 1991. Reprinted by permission of the author.

Alison Luterman: "Dancing With Pan" originally appeared in *Shadow Play,* Divine Fool Press. Reprinted by permission of the author.

Lisa Martinovic: "Next Time" originally appeared in *Adventures in Coming Alive:* New Paradigm Productions, 1993. Reprinted by permission of the author.

Patricia Monaghan: "Procedure for Reclaiming the Self" originally appeared in *Seasons of the Witch:* Delphi Press, 1992. Reprinted by permission of the author.

Cindy Rosmus: "Mikey's Dad" originally appeared in *The North American Review:* March, 1991. Reprinted by permission of the author.

Gianna Russo: "Mr. and Mrs. Jack Sprat" originally appeared in *New CollAge:* Volume 20, Issue 3, 1982. Reprinted by permission of the author.

Sheryl St. Germain: "Addiction" originally appeared in *The Taos Review:* Number 3, 1990. Reprinted by permission of the author.

Alison Stone: "Just Like Sister Ray Said" originally appeared in the *New York Quarterly:* October 1992. Reprinted by permission of the author.

Michelle M. Tokarczyk: "To A.A." and "A Favor" originally appeared in *The House I'm Running Away From:* West End Press, 1989. Reprinted by permission of the author.

Cheryl Townsend: "Used To" originally appeared in *Art! Mag:* April, 1986. Reprinted by permission of the author.

For Lyman, whose gentle
and courageous spirit
is teaching me to trust at last.

Introduction

Sleeping with Dionysus:
Women, Ecstasy and Addiction

For many women physical passion and chemical abuse seem inextricably intertwined. As children we are taught that our sexuality is somehow bad or wrong. Some of us were sexually abused. In adolescence we often discover that drinking and/or drugging is the magic potion which releases our inhibitions so we are able to more easily act on our desires or to allow ourselves to feel them in the first place. Other women take solace in food or extreme dependency on other people. Eventually what seemed like such a miraculous aphrodisiac may become a substitute for love, crowding out the possibility of healthy love relationships—with partners, with ourselves, with the world around us and with the Sacred.

Like Ariadne of Greek myth, we become wed to the god of ecstasy. Ariadne, the lover of Dionysus was originally not merely the partner of the god of wine and revelry, but a goddess in her own right. Her name means "very holy," and in ancient Crete she was worshipped by women as the goddess of the underworld and germination. She was the Earth Mother. When the Greeks conquered Crete, they suppressed worship of Ariadne by demoting her from goddess to mortal woman and incorporating her into their own mythology.

According to the Greek revised version of the tale, Ariadne had been a very beautiful and very human princess of Crete, betrayed by her lover Theseus. They met when Theseus, a mortal from Athens, volunteered to kill the Minotaur, a half-bull/half-human monster which lived in a labyrinth beneath the city. No man had survived such an attempt before.

From the first time she saw him, Ariadne was attracted to Theseus and decided to assist him if he would take her to Athens and marry her. When he agreed, she gave him a ball of twine and told him to tie the end to the door at the entrance of the maze, unwinding the string as he worked his way toward the center. To find his way back to safety, all he would have to do was to follow the string and reverse his steps. Aided by Ariadne's cleverness, he killed the Minotaur and took her on his ship sailing toward Athens.

On the journey, the lovers made port in Naxos and debarked. As soon as Ariadne fell asleep on shore, Theseus, who had no more use for her cleverness, abandoned her and sailed off on his own. When Ariadne awakened and found herself deserted, she grieved—until Dionysus appeared. He was a savior/destroyer god who wandered the world with his female attendants and panthers. Dionysus was the god who had brought the Greeks agriculture, art and drama as well as wine. He represented the dual nature of intoxication, and his mystery was the mystery of mad despair and of ecstasy.

When Dionysus found Ariadne on Naxos, he fell in love with her and married her. In some stories, he gave her a crown, and when she died, he tossed that crown up to the heavens where it shines today. According to other versions of the legend, he took Ariadne, herself, with him to the heavens where she became immortalized—transformed into a goddess through *his* efforts.

Given the Greeks' goal to suppress the religion of the goddess worshippers and the dual nature of Dionysus' character, it isn't surprising that other, more popular variations of the story take a more sinister turn. These say that Dionysus and Ariadne were lovers in Crete until Theseus kidnaped her. In the version recounted in The Odyssey, when Theseus later abandoned Ariadne on the island, Dionysus ordered her killed. In another version she hanged herself, and in yet another account she became pregnant and died the instant before she was able to give birth to the child fathered by Dionysus before her abduction. The god of wine who had the power to immortalize Ariadne also had the power to destroy her or compel her to destroy herself.

In classical art the wine god was often portrayed surrounded by women called Maenads. In his worship in Greece, he was served by priestesses. When a woman was initiated into the mysteries of Dionysus, she entered into a sacred marriage with the god, identifying completely with Ariadne. These women had no formal temples; instead, they worshipped their god in the wilderness.

There they celebrated Dionysus with drunkenness, orgies and nakedness, with music and movement, sexuality and intoxication. Their rituals could be incredibly dark when ecstasy turned to raging, brutal frenzy. Sometimes these priestesses of Dionysus became "possessed" with him and became wild women, tearing apart sacrificial victims. It was rumored that they even ate their victims' flesh in a bloody feast.

Ariadne, the mortal woman, and the Maenads who took on her identity, wanted union with a God. People today who become dependent on alcohol or drugs often do so in a misguided attempt to slake their thirst for the Divine, according to Matthew Fox, an eminent Catholic theologian, and many chemical dependency experts.

Male-dominated culture has worked for thousands of years to strip women of our awareness of the holy, of the Goddess inside of us, to suppress our sexuality and to divorce our spirituality from our bodies. We are taught to be ashamed of ourselves and our ecstatic feelings. Western religious tradition excludes women from full participation and sometimes damns us solely because of our sex. In order to truly connect with the Divine we are told we must deny our physical selves.

Because of this, women may be especially vulnerable to seeking chemical means, food or "love addiction" to alter consciousness. By sleeping with Dionysus we initially feel as though we were transported to the heavens and made goddesses. We feel holy again, whole. When we become Maenads through our intoxication, we are at last able to catch a glimpse of our own primal wildness, our Goddess energy. We feel uninhibited, ecstatic; we are able to sing and to dance, to laugh and to weep without wondering what other people are thinking. We are able to remove the stiff and ill-fitting clothing society has forced us to wear in the form of people-pleasing personas.

And then the ritual marriage turns dark. Our drinking, drugging, eating or compulsive relationships unleash incredible amounts of destructive anger. We rage; we become frenzied. Our fury from past pain mounts and, with it, our capacity for violence. If we remain the wine god's lover, our fate will be the same as Ariadne's in the two most misogynist versions of her tale. We will either turn the rage inward, destroying ourselves through madness, suicide or illness, or we will be killed by Dionysus' hit man in the form of an under-the-influence accident or at the hands of an abusive lover.

Our recovery process must involve divorcing Dionysus and reconnecting with the Sacred which lives within each one of us. When we return Ariadne to her original position as Earth Goddess rather than victim and recognize that she lives in each one of us, we no longer feel compelled to seek out Dionysus in the form of chemicals, food or relationships to experience ecstatic connection. We begin to embrace and express our primal feminine energy. We have the choice of how and when to express it and can decide to do that in constructive and creative ways. We become lovers not only of sexual partners, but of ourselves, the world and the Divine. Our past experience with addiction becomes the catalyst for the germination of our wholeness.

The short stories, poems and memoirs gathered for this book parallel Ariadne's journey from childhood in her father's house, through her unfulfilling relationships with Theseus, her dance with Dionysus and eventually her homecoming to self. The women who wrote them share their experience of addiction and recovery in the hope that others will make the healing journey within as they have.

Addiction

by Celia Stuart-Powels

It's hard
to understand the
attraction now.
But I think it
was like being
the hunter
and the
prey.

The search, the
aim, the hit:
flash of red blood.
The moment:
lost and crumpling
in complete
release/abandonment.
The ecstasy of
dying.

And then...
the hunt began
again,
and again the
dying.

I

A Maenad's Childhood

When I Remember

by Andrea Kelly

Sometimes
it boils to the surface,
something buried deep,
trying to breathe;

or pops
like a brain cell
lost in the roar
of an empty bottle.

By the speckled light
of a plastic conch
plugged into my bedroom wall,
I see my mother.
Her hand sifts my hair.

"Your father..." she begins,
and spins for herself
a soft web of reasons.

Between sleeping and waking,
I slipped through her fingers
to follow in his footsteps.

Trespass

by Catherine Gammon

A woman picks up a younger man—in a bar. A passion. He lives with her—after three weeks she is dead. There is no third party. No witness. Only the man and the death. This is the story. Stop here. There is no solution.

Intervention—she wishes to intervene. In her personal history. In the life surrounding her. In the future. She would like to go back to that time when she was a child in Los Angeles riding with her father in the car at night and he pulled over to the curb and got out and in the darkness pissed against a tree. She would like to stop there and say little girl, don't be afraid, your father's drunk and it's not your fault. She would like to go back and warn the child, herself, you're not crazy, your father's lying, don't blame him, don't forget what you know, don't let your mother pretend—don't lose track of your life for their sakes. She would like to go back and stand up to those people, the mother, the father, and speak the truth, and force them to speak it. She would like to go back and find the truth. But she is a ghost in that past, as for you as I write, as you read (because I have told you), she is a ghost already.

This will have been a cold story. (Lexical citations are derived from the *American Heritage Dictionary of the English Language,* Houghton Mifflin, 1981.) It was a hot night but the woman was cold. Cold inside her skin. She could feel the shivering start and lost her power of concentration. She had been reading and put the book face down on the nightstand. In the bar she saw the man—dark-haired, lean, and beautiful. He was looking at her. He was watching the door and didn't move his eyes from her as she walked in. He didn't smile. He was something out of a movie. A silent movie. Where everything was in the seeing, in the look. She watched him and didn't smile. She ordered a bourbon and forgot him, then saw him in the mirror. He stood next to her. They leaned together against the bar. She felt his breath against her shoulder—briefly, passing, he turned around, leaned back into his elbows and looked for her face. She gave it to him: this is my face.

On reading Derrida: She picked him up in a bookstore. She brought him home. Three weeks later she was dead. She also brought home Lao Tzu, Thomas Merton (the wisdom of the desert), Kierkegaard (either/or, volume one), and the *Bhagavad Gita*. But it was Derrida who killed her (dissemination) because it was Derrida she began to read and left abandoned on her night table when she got up and got dressed and went down to the corner for a drink.

She did not like his face in the mirror. He sensed this. In the mirror his face was false. She averted her eyes from his mirror face. He was careful from then on not to meet her face in mirrors.

Bourbon had been her father's drink. She rode beside him in the car, just the two of them. He reached his hand into his pocket, pulled out a pint, drank from the bottle, left hand still at the wheel. She would see this image clearly, in her memory, never knew if it was once or many times she saw it, knew it didn't matter, the thing itself was constant and repeated, whether seen by her or not. He drank far more than her mother knew, more than her mother either could or would imagine. With her drinker's heart she knew this, then and now.

Intervene: *1.To enter or occur extraneously. 2.To come, appear, or lie between two things. 3.To occur or come between two periods or points of time. 4.To come in or between so as to hinder or modify. 5.To interfere, usually through force or threat of force in the affairs of another nation. 6.Law. To enter into a suit as a third party for the protection of an alleged interest. [Latin intervenire, to come between: inter-, between + venire, to come (see* **gwa-** *in Appendix of Indo-European Roots*).]*

They made love and slept and ate and drank and made love and slept and drank. They did as little as possible of what had to be done: they excluded everything. She called in sick and unplugged the phone. She brought the mail up and didn't open it. No one knew where to find him. He had nothing and no one to leave.

She would like to return to the past to which she can't return. She would like to find answers to questions to which she can find no answers. She would like to say to her mother: I was a child. I didn't know the word pissed. Pissed is a word that protects me, now, from the darkness and the fear when Daddy stopped the car and left me and leaned against a tree. I followed him. (Did I?) He yelled at me. (Did he?) How long did I sit alone in the car before I got out? (Was he too sick to yell at me? Was he sick, or only pissing?) Why do I remember this? So much and so little? I remember the darkness and the night—the tree—fear. I remember, maybe, that Daddy was crying.

She woke up one morning and saw the man had become a loathsome bug. His face, which had been so beautiful, was suddenly cunning and sly. He wore his mirror face beside her, and she recoiled. She lit a cigarette. He spoke to her. She didn't understand the words. He asked her a question. She began to answer it. He asked another question. She drew back farther. Every question he asked her pulled her farther from the original question, and pulled her farther away from herself and from him. He became ugly. She got up from the bed screaming. She grabbed the nearest thing to hand and threw it back across the room at him. It was the book she had been reading the night they met. He followed her into the bathroom. In the mirror he was beautiful. He pounded his hand against her image—his image. The mirror shattered. His hand bled, dripping down into the sink. She stood frozen, looking: the white sink cold and gleaming—tiny mirrors glittering and in the bigger shards her face—his bright dark blood. They both stood arrested—as if suddenly sober: time suspended, battle done—white, red, silver. She pulled a towel down and wrapped his hand.

In the bar they had talked about political violence: Star Wars, apartheid, Central America, intervention. In bed they shut the world out. They saw the sun and shadows move across the floor. When they got restless she connected the phone and called out for cigarettes, liquor, and food. There is no third party. They were alone.

In Los Angeles in some neighborhoods the trees are planted in a narrow strip of grass that runs along the curb, between the street and the sidewalk, one tree per lot. It was an old neighborhood, they were old lots. It was a big tree, relatively speaking. Not young and skinny like the tree outside their own house. Not thicker than a person like the trees she knows now in the East. But relatively speaking, a big tree. As big around as her father's leg, maybe, his thigh, maybe a little bigger. Yes, she got out of the car. She sees him clearly, leaning in the night against the tree. More than this she has never remembered. Only the mood of shame and fear and the knowledge that she saw what she was not supposed to see. There is no one to speak for her. She wants to intervene on her own behalf. She wants to say wait, this is not an isolated incident, this is important—wants to shake the man, the sick drunk man against the tree, lean and beautiful, dark-haired and fair-skinned in the moonlight. But she is inventing the moonlight. She is looking at her lover's dark eyes, his tousled hair—brown, almost black, like her father's. She is living in the smell of old bourbon, Camel cigarettes, and sweat—her father's smells— and sex, the dirty sheets. Don't forget, she wants to cry—don't let this little girl forget—and wants to pull him away from the tree and slap him and push him down to the ground, to his knees, to force him to cry—to cry so that he'll remember, so she will remember, so she'll know what really happened, what she saw, what she felt, and before that, in the car, and when he stopped the car, and before he started it again, and later, when they got home, when they faced her mother, and when they hid—wants to pull her father around and pound his chest, make fists and beat his chest, naked, hairless, like her lover's, and cry, you lied to her, all her life you lied, don't you know what you did?—she'll think she's crazy because you're her father and you lied—it's not what you did—she doesn't know what you did—it's that you lied — look at her—she's seen you lying and you're her father and when you lie there is no truth— but it's her lover's chest she's pounding and while she weeps he holds her wrists, waiting for the screaming and weeping to pass, waiting to let loose his grip and pull her head to his shoulder to soothe her and stroke her head, her hair, when she will weep more quietly against his skin.

> **Gwa-**. *Also gwem-. To go, come. 1.Germanic *kuman in: a.Old English cuman, to come: COME; b.Germanic *kuma-, he who comes, a guest, in compound *wil-kuma-, a desirable guest (*wil-, desirable; see* **wel-***), in Old English wilcuma, a welcome guest, and wilcume, the greeting of welcome: WELCOME; c.compound *bi-kuman, to arrive, come to be (*bi-, intensive prefix: be-), in Old English becuman, to become: BECOME.*

The word pissed is an intervention. Language is an intervention. In her mouth all speech intervenes. In her mind words come between—hinder and modify, interfere, usually by force or threat of force, enter into suit, allege interest, attempt protection. They come, they appear, they lie between—they lie. Extraneous, they enter. Like this lover, this stranger in her body.

She woke up. She felt a body in the bed behind her, breathing against her neck. She shivered and pulled away, curling into herself. Her skin crawled. Lavender light came in from the street in slivers that outlined the desk, the lamp, the bookshelf, the door. Desk. Lamp. Bookshelf. Door. She couldn't identify them. She didn't know the room. It was too dark. The lavender edges of things gave back no information. She pulled the sticky sheet tighter around her shoulder and shivered in her skin. She felt her heartbeat, fast and fluttery, doing doubletime and depthless. Her skin was cold and clammy. The lavender outlines began to move in the room, sinuous and swirling, became cartoon shapes, illegible words written in air, welcome, whispering, grasses twitching, wild eyes watching from the other side of the night. Her mind was clear. She knew she was awake. She knew these visions were in her mind, projected into the room. She wanted to see what would come next. But they scared her. She closed her eyes and saw nothing. She opened her eyes and saw the wild lights. She closed her eyes and rolled away to the stranger's body. If she looked at him she would see a stranger's face and hallucinate love. She lay there, stiff, cold, curled up against him. She felt her heart beat in her chest, fast and shallow. She took deep, slow breaths. She kept her eyes closed. She waited. She expected to die. The night went on.

He had become a loathsome bug. His hand bled. They were out of booze. She tried to make coffee but she was trembling—the blood, the breaking glass, the screaming—the shock of seeing his face so ugly. And maybe too much bourbon, she thought. She didn't know what day it was, how long he'd been here, she wasn't sure she knew his name. But the sight of his blood had made her tender. She leaned over him in the bright reading light next to the bed and painstakingly with shaking hands and a tweezer pulled out slivers of glass. They called the liquor store for vodka to wash his wounds and to celebrate the fact that it wasn't Sunday.

According to Bachelard (the psychoanalysis of fire) alcohol is a creator of language. It enriches the vocabulary and frees the syntax. The alcoholic unconscious is a profound reality. Alcohol does not simply stimulate mental potentialities, it creates them. Alcohol incorporates itself with that which is striving to express itself. These are Bachelard's words, approximately as translated into English by Alan C.M. Ross. What Bachelard does not say—or if he says it, she failed to notice, or if she noticed, the caution eluded her—is that for some people this alcoholic incorporation is irreversible (incorporate: to unite with or blend indistinguishably into something already in existence; to give substance or material form to; embody), the exchange vampiric, Faustian; that for such people, to enact this bargain (given, not chosen) is to die or to live in hell.

In her nightmare her father is in the bed with her, the breath on her neck is her father's breath, the leg against her leg her father's leg, the heat and wetness in her body for her father's pleasure, the searching fingers her father's fingers, the erection moving against her skin, against her bottom, the back of her thighs, her inner thighs in search of welcome, her father's. In her nightmare she wakes up screaming, but in reality her lover is coming into her and when she starts to scream he pushes her head into the pillow until their lovemaking is done. In her nightmare her father was in the bed wrapped in sheets and she stroked him, half-erect. In her nightmare he was an old man, the man he was just before he died. She was asking for information, stroking and waiting, cajoling, until a rush of potency scared her and she withdrew her hand. "Did you ever make me do this?" she asked, and he told her once, that night he got her loaded. "Did you get me loaded?" she asked, and already in her nightmare she saw the bottle on a chair in the other bedroom where her mother sat in bed, the way she did every morning, reading prayers. In her nightmare a third person was in the bed with her and her father—a shadowy person, almost no one. In her nightmare her father pressed himself against her from behind and she felt his probing fingers. In reality at the age of four she was suddenly afraid of the dark. In reality whatever happened her father will remember nothing. This is the moment in which she would like to intervene. But to intervene is to wake herself, and in reality she screamed. She remembered nothing of reality, only the nightmare, and pressed against the pillow by the violent hand of a stranger, unable to breathe and heaving under the effort and sweat of his young body, she tasted her own juices, and vodka, and blood against her cheek.

> **Wel-**. *To wish, will. 1.Germanic, *wel- in Old English wel, well ("according to one's wish"): WELL 2.Germanic *welon- in Old English wela, weola, well-being, riches: WEAL (WEALTH). 3.Germanic *wiljon- in Old English willa, desire, will power: WILL. 4.Germanic *wil(l)ian in Old English wyllan, to desire: WILL, NILL. 5.Germanic compound *wil-kuma (see* **gwa-***). 6.0-grade form wol- in Germanic *wal- in Frankish *wala, well: GALA, GALLANT, GALLOP, WALLOP. 7.Basic form *wel- in Latin velle, to wish, will: VOLITION, VOLUNTARY, BENEVOLENT, MALEVOLENT. 8.Suffixed form *wel-up in Latin voluptas, pleasure.*

Freud is no help. Freud said the little girls desired the unthinkable and repressed the desire. Recent scholars say the fathers did the unthinkable and Freud repressed the facts. The debate continues. She will find no answer: there is no solution in theory, her mother knows nothing, and her father is dead. Her triangle can be unraveled only by opening it up in time. But she is out of time.

The delivery boy from the liquor store rang the bell for 5-E as he had done almost every day for three weeks. The first morning they were laughing and wrapped in sheets. The man said they were having a honeymoon, they expected to see a lot of him, and gave him a ten-dollar tip. At first they ordered bourbon, then they switched to vodka. Sometimes he brought them one bottle, sometimes two. At first they paid with cash, later with checks. The boss said he knew the woman a couple of years, her checks had always been good, At first the delivery boy liked going to them—they were happy and sexy to look at and generous with the money. They gave him an extra five dollars to stop at the corner and bring them a carton each of Marlboros and Camels. They always buzzed him up right away and let him inside when they opened the door, they were nice with him—in fact, they excited him. But rapidly he decided they were pigs. The air in the apartment was stale and stank of something skunklike and deadly. Their faces became ashen and their eyes dark-hollowed. They were like junkies, he told the boss. The tips dried up. The woman reeked of ammonia, as if it came oozing out her skin. Once on the other side of their door he heard screaming that suddenly stopped. The man came to meet him alone, wearing jeans and a khaki shirt, unbuttoned. His skin was scratched and bleeding. The check he gave him was crumpled and almost torn. It was the woman's check. Her handwriting was illegible. The man gave him an extra dollar to carry down a bag of empties. "Don't come back," he said. "No matter what we tell you, promise you—don't come back." But he had come back. When they called and gave the boss an order, he had no choice but to go. Every day then he dreaded them. Until the morning when he stood on the stoop ringing and got no answer. He was carrying two quarts of cheap vodka and a carton each of Camels and Marlboros. He rang and rang. He went back to the store and told the boss. "I spent twenty-four bucks on cigarettes for those people," he said. "That's your problem," the boss said. "They're killing each other," the boy said, and the boss said that wasn't his business, as long as the checks were good. The boy walked out. He came back to the building and rang for the super. They went up together. The super pounded. There was no answer. He yelled, he said, "We're coming in." They waited. Slowly, the super unlocked the door. The boy gagged on the threshold. The skunk smell was overpowering, and all the human fluid smells, and fear. The boy crossed himself in the presence of what he knew was death. Neither he nor the super went in.

Replete and fearful—feeling exists but she is willing to know it only in the mind. She thinks she wants illumination, reality, the absence of deceit, but she is too absent from herself, too well protected. She is too old, she thinks, to wait for miracles. But pleasure is terror: If I take a knife to him, she wonders, will he give me back the truth?

She would like to intervene. Here perhaps: She had been reading for several hours when she began to get an inkling of the method and laughed out loud. She realized she would be too stimulated to sleep. She put the book down on the night-stand. Or here: He wore an overcoat in houndstooth plaid, black and ivory. Invented like the moonlight. Or not. He gave her a drink from his bottle. She asked for more. He gave it to her: Don't tell your mother. Later he was crying.

In a mirror, across the room, the man: huddled, so small and naked as almost to be invisible—he, who had been so beautiful. In the mirror, a bloody sheet, and everywhere the traces of its passage. In the mirror, his hands bloody, his chest, his skin cut and torn. In the mirror, in his lap, in his bloody hands, a telephone—suddenly familiar. He remembers where he is. They were sitting in separate corners, each with a bottle. The blood surprises him.

Here and now: She wishes to speak. Too much is missing. Nothing is right yet. Her story is not complete. There is more to say: I am a little girl who lives in a jail. Outside a neighbor is yelling at a dog to shut up. Every day she yells at the dog to shut up. I hate it when she yells at the dog to shut up. I also hate the dog. Most of the time I ignore the yelling neighbor and the dog. I let my jailer hate the yelling neighbor and the dog. Most of the time I ignore everything. I live in a dark jail. I came into this jail when I was a little girl and I'm still a little girl. I am alone in the house. Most of the time I like being alone in the house. In the house alone I act our fairy tales—mostly Cinderella—my favorite part is when she buries her head in her arms and cries on the bench. The coffee table is just the size of the bench in my picture book and I act it all out up to the part where she weeps because her wicked stepsisters have ripped up her dress and she can't go to the ball—up to the part where she weeps crying on the bench—right before the fairy godmother comes. I am the little girl crying, waiting for the fairy godmother to come and send her off to the ball and the handsome prince and the triumph over the wicked stepsisters and the happiness ever after. That's how old I really am, in my heart. And there's more to say. There will always be more to say.

For a while they watch television, soap operas, anything. She soaks in the bathtub, sleeping. He pulls her up by the hair. She holds on to his shoulders, her grip is slippery, she falls. Water splashes. They have bruises. In the tub they examine each other's bruises. Next they study the scars. His hand bleeds. Together they take time to dream. They can leave this city. They can go anywhere. They don't have to live like this. They are free. The sun is coming up. The little bit of sky out her window is almost blue. She lights a Marlboro and watches the smoke blown to nothing by the fan. The ash falls, she scatters it away.

Bad Girl

by Devon Vose

Will I always
be the bad girl
telling dirty
stories they
don't want to hear.

Are You Ever Going to Be Thin?

by Jennifer Semple Siegel

Oct. 1958

Dear Cuddles,

Happy birthday! So you are eight years old. Such a little lady, I hear. Buy something pretty (not candy) with the enclosed check. You're my little cuddler, and I want you to be happy.

Are you still fat? Your Nana told me she took you to Dr. Noonan for your check-up and he said you had to lose 10 lbs. by Xmas. Sweetheart, that's only two and a half months away and you know how Santa don't like to give presents to little fat girls. I'm sure he wants to bring you many pretty dresses but his elves don't know how to make Lane Bryant sizes. Besides, how would Santa deliver all those big clothes?

Saw Hilda today. Remember her? She went on a crash diet last year and lost 50 lbs. in two months. Now she's gained it all back and then some. So sad. You don't want to be big like her. I hope you can lose that awful fat by Xmas.

Well, must run. Have a brunch date with Vesta. We're going to the pancake place. I know how you like their Pigs-in-a-Blanket. Maybe if you're thin next summer you can come to California and I'll take you there. And then we can cuddle.

Love to Nana and Pappa.

Love,
Your Auntie

No, you *cannot* have any more popcorn. If you want anything else, there's celery and carrots in the fridge. I sliced them just for you. If you don't eat them, I'll just have to throw them out, and we can't afford to waste good food. How many times do I have to tell you Pappa don't make very much on Social Security? You know what Dr. Noonan says: you got to eat vegetables and lean meat and stay away from all that butter, sugar, and starch. I don't CARE what Dr. Noonan weighs. He's a man and it don't matter what HE weighs. But you're a girl, and men, even fat ones, don't like fat girls. And if you don't lose all that weight, you'll *never* catch a husband. And if you get too fat, you'll get lazy. I see it already. Your room looks like a pigsty. Why, I found all those candy wrappers and sunflower seed shells everywhere. Is that how you spent your birthday money?

Of course, your mama still loves you. Maybe the present got lost in the mail. These things happen sometimes. I just think it wouldn't be a good idea to call her right now. Auntie says your mama's been feelin' a little punk lately and needs her rest. Maybe at Christmas.

Must you kids always fight? Danny, you go sit in the swivel chair. Sammy, you wash those dishes or else. Sammy! You heard me! Danny! I'm going to send you home if you don't stop calling your cousin names. And you, young lady, stop your whining. Danny don't mean nothing. He's just foolin' you. You take everything so serious. And *you*, shut up! Sammy, get into the kitchen!

Here, I'll dry. Oh, this towel's soggy. Honey, hand me that one next to you. Don't pay no mind to Danny. Boys will be boys. If he didn't like you, he wouldn't say nothing to you. But, you know, he's just saying what others are thinking. Just because most people don't say nothing doesn't mean they don't notice. They got eyes, you know. Don't you want to grow up and have a nice husband and family? This pot's got goo on it; do it over. How many times do I have to tell you about your sloppy ways? I'm just trying to raise you right. Make up for what happened to your mother. And you're just like your mama, except she wasn't fat. And look where it got her. Time to change the rinse water. See that soap scum on the top? You don't want to get all of us sick, do you?

Did you take your pill yet? I don't *care* if it keeps you up at night. Besides, Dr. Noonan can give you a pill to make you sleep. I'll call him today. *It is very important you take those pills*. They'll curb that monstrous appetite of yours.

Don't forget to write Auntie the "thank you" note. Here it is, only one month 'til Christmas, and you haven't even thanked her for your birthday present yet. Whatever is going to become of you?

You have to wait twenty minutes before you can eat. Even lettuce. You have to let the pill work first so you don't go out of control. Girl, you sure could use some self-control these days. You know, Gluttony is a mortal sin. A *capital* sin. The worst kind. Except for LUST, but you're too young to know about that. You'll go to hell for sure if you don't stop stuffing yourself. I just don't know what to do about you. If you keep on going the way you're going, they'll need a derrick to carry you around. Tsk, tsk.

Take your pill; eat your lettuce; don't wear that—it's too tight—your belly hangs out; drink your water, no, you can't have any pop, it's pure sugar; don't jiggle your butt like that; do you really think those nigger pants look good on you! If you insist on eating Chicken Noodle soup all the time, you will have to learn to light the pilot—I'm tired of washing out the coffee pot after every other meal; you know you can't buy a boy's bike—because the bar might hurt your bubo—I can't tell you how, you're too young—no, you haven't done nothing wrong; Dr. Noonan says you can't eat peanut butter until you lose three more pounds; don't fight with your cousins and never tattle on no one—it don't look good; always listen to the Sisters, they know what's best for your soul; by next year, you'll need a girdle for sure and maybe even a bra; if Father Salvatore says no more black patent leather shoes, then he must have a good reason—how would I know, you just obey and don't ask questions; I think it's time you stopped sleeping with your grandpa—no, you haven't done nothing wrong, it's just time you start staying in your own bed at night; go to Mass; go to Confession; say a rosary; say "now I lay me down to sleep, I pray the Lord my soul to keep, if I should die before I wake, I pray the Lord my soul to take—there are four corners on my bed, there are four angels overhead—Matthew, Mark, Luke, and John, bless this bed that I lay on"; Jesus loves all the little children, even little chubby ones, but he likes the humble ones the best; yes, you are my favorite child—I always like the one I'm with the best; be careful around your cousins, especially Danny—no, you haven't done nothing wrong—no, I can't tell you what to watch for, you're too young—just be careful; don't eat chocolate, you'll break out in pimples, maybe not right away, but when you get older; where on earth did you get that peanut butter cup?; for God's sake, are you EVER going to be thin?

Oct. 1962

Dear Little Cuddler,

I guess you're not so little anymore. Twelve already.

I hear you're thin again. I'm so proud of you! Now you can buy some pretty skinny dresses with the enclosed check.

I'm looking forward to your visit next summer. We'll go to Farmer's Market for enchiladas and Humphrey's Bakery for a fancy cake. Remember how much you liked Farmer's Market? Now that you're thin, we can enjoy nice restaurants, not that awful diet food you had to eat for three months. So don't get fat in the next nine months. I know you can keep the weight off because your Nana says the thyroid and diet pills are working just fine. Sorry to hear about Dr. Noonan. Your Nana said it was a heart attack but I hear your new doctor is young & cute. Watch out! (ha, ha).

Your boyfriend Jimmy sounds like a very nice boy. Does he know you like him?

Saw your mother the other day. She came out from the valley for a visit, and we went to lunch at the Hungry Tiger. She eats like a bird! She's got a new boyfriend, wonder if she'll marry this one. Sounds nice enough, though. Sells used cars and plays horn in a jazz band where your mama used to work. She invited me to the club on Fri. nite, but I already got a date with Bob and Andy—they're kind of swishy, I know, but they've got a beautiful new home in Beverly Hills. They asked about you. Your mama looked real good, good color, she says she's not drinking anymore. Still smokes like a stack, though. She asked about you and wonders why you don't answer her letters. Said she was going to send you a nice birthday present. Did she?

Had Vesta, Dame, Hilda and Jack over for dinner last week. Poor Hilda. She must weigh over 300 lbs. now. I grilled a thick, juicy steak and tossed a nice, big salad with homemade ranch dressing and baked some gigantic Idahos in the oven. Served with sour cream and chives. For dessert, we had New York style cheesecake with cherries. They all loved it! Got so many compliments. Wish you could have been here to enjoy it.

Donald and I are going to Vegas in two weeks. You remember Donald, don't you? I borrowed his Cadillac one time when you were 4 and you peed all over the front seat. I was absolutely mortified! It's a wonder he still speaks to me. You know, you never do get rid of that smell. Anyway, Donald owns part of a casino in Carson City and has to settle some business there. So he invited me along and we'll hit some of the big casinos and shows in Vegas. Will send you a pretty card.

Tell me what you'd like to do next summer so I can plan our itinerary. I'm planning a six-week cruise to Australia in August and September so plan to come in June. Would you like to see the La Brea Tar Pits and Forest Lawn? I know you'll want to go to Disneyland and Knotts Berry Farm.

I look forward to cuddling with my skinny little cuddler.

Love to Nana and Pappa.

Love,

Your Auntie

Honey, I just don't think that's the right dress for you. You can't wear such a bright red to school, the nuns would absolutely die. It's cut too skimpy, and you're only twelve. You'll have boys all over you. No, you haven't done nothing wrong, it's just that dresses cut like this one attract certain boys and you don't want to put yourself in a predicament. I think it means "situation." No, I can't tell you any more—you're too young. How about this nice linen navy? Oh, hell, we'll look for dresses later. Let's go over to lingerie, your bra is cutting into your midriff.

Let's see...36 B, 36 C, 38 A, 38 B—ah, here we are, 38 C. It is not too big. You have to buy bras that hook on the first clasp so you don't outgrow them right away. How many times do I have to tell you that?

For God's sake, can't we ever go shopping without all this hassle? I'm all in. Let's go for a snack.

Are you sure you really want those fries? Why not just a loose meat sandwich and a root beer float? I hate all that old fried stuff. Oh, okay. You're keeping the weight off pretty good so I guess it's okay, just this once. I'll just have a root beer and a loose meat with a dill slice.

I have to talk to you anyway without your Pappa around. No, you haven't done nothing wrong, I just want to talk girl stuff with you. Soon, you're going to be a woman, and you have to know some things...How did you know about that, anyway? Humph, I never did like that Charlene friend of yours anyway.

Pass the ketchup. Bought a kit for you. Comes with a booklet, a special belt, and, you know, pads. You'll know what to do when the time comes. Just read the instructions.

Where on earth did you ever hear about tampons? Under no circumstances are you to use tampons. Because they'll hurt your bubo, and I can't tell you why. You're still too young. Just do as I say.

Don't gobble your food like a pig and do you really need that big glob of ketchup on your plate?

Ironing

by Madelyn Camrud

On those long days, summer afternoons,
in the turquoise, wainscoted porch, I stood
leaning over the board, steaming
the rickrack on Mother's aprons.
Drapes with peonies dressed
windows to the floor. I wanted to raise
a tall bottle, and swirl wine
down my throat, until I floated
into chasms where rivers rose
and fell, taking me in
the way a song fills
a mouth then leaves, breath
by breath. At times,

I wanted to go that far
to meet the man I imagined,
the one who resembled Jon,
but was far more attractive.
I gazed the half-mile to the mailbox
and pictured his lips sealing
a letter. Setting
the iron on its heel,
I went to the window and pressed
my lips against the frame's smooth,
pink, enamel. His arms closed
like warm darkness around me
as we kissed, then he ushered me
down a long hall and pushed me, gently,
to my knees. My body spilled
like milk onto a cushion
and we met, inside that moment,
as if at the end of
or inside things there was an answer.

Lighter Fluid

by Paula Legendre

When I was sixteen and a virgin, I thought about what I would do if I were raped. Given a choice of fight and be killed or give up my precious treasure to a stranger, I always believed that putting up a fight and its life-threatening consequences would be preferable.

Five years later, I used that precious treasure at every opportunity to purchase something more important, something I had left behind when I traveled west from Colorado for a summer job—security. But I spent more that summer than I received, and even now that seventeen years have passed, I know that the account will never be closed.

Blood greeted me as I stepped off the airplane that May at the San Francisco airport. Hurrying to the restroom, I tried to dab at the damage this cabernet-colored discharge had wrought, and at the same time, wondered at its cause. Could I be pregnant? It wasn't time for my period. What was happening to me? I didn't know a soul. I pondered these things as the Greyhound bus made its way over the Bay Bridge and through the brown hills to Livermore, California, where I was to work as an engineering assistant.

Up until then, I had been excited about the prospect of leaving Colorado for the first time to work an hour away from San Francisco. This was to be Liberation Summer, the summer of 1976, when the rest of the nation was celebrating its bicentennial. I couldn't wait to get away from home and start living my own life.

That spring semester, too, had been particularly difficult. Working two part-time jobs that meant half-time employment and taking 18 hours of junior-level engineering courses had exhausted me. My mother kept warning me of a nervous break-down, and I labored through that grueling spring just to show her, always looking for her elusive vote of approval. Of course, I didn't get it. Even as I was inducted into Mortar Board, the most prestigious honor society on the University of Colorado campus, I kept hearing her voice of doom, "I'm still afraid that you're heading toward that nervous breakdown." Honor soci-eties, good grades, and unceasing work—I guessed only having that nervous breakdown would have made her happy.

Well, California would be a clean start. Certainly, it had been for the millions of others who had immigrated before me. The blood at the airport, however, soiled what was to be a new beginning.

The kicked-in door of the house in which I would be rent-ing a room was not reassuring either. Knocking several times on that bashed-in harvest green door, I waited while the sounds of lovemaking subsided before a disheveled woman and her frustrated boyfriend invited me in.

By that summer, I was no stranger to sex. I'd given up my virginity fifteen months earlier in an act of protest against my father. Anger was the match that lit the lighter fluid poured over that first penetration, and I remember thinking, was this all? Had I put off my steady of two years by doing everything else for such an anti-climax? What a waste of energy it had all been.

I found, however, once the fire of sexual addiction and anger had been lit, I was powerless to put it out. I needed my daily orgasm from Chuck. The sex, however, didn't put out my anger against my father. It grew until it encompassed Chuck, too.

Chuck had been my protector. Faced with having him by my side or attending classes alone, and often as the only female, I clung to him. The relationship soured when my mother "adopted" Chuck as her third son. Poor Chuck. Poor me. I never could compete against my three siblings—now with Chuck in the picture, Mom's approval seemed infinitely less attainable. Anyway, with her help, Chuck had been banished that summer to Alaska. As much as I thought I despised him (an emotion that actually disguised my jealousy of him), I desperately missed his companionship out in California.

I quickly discovered blood and sex were not the only things tainting the California landscape. Wine was everywhere. It was in the vineyards—twenty minutes of vineyards—that lined the road that I walked to work. One mile of twisted branches sprouting out of the earth, the green leaves making the distant brown hills appear less dry. I had never seen a grape arbor before, and the gnarled branches soon symbolized my life as a transplanted Coloradan. The grapes from this vineyard graced the communion tables of Catholic churches through America, I found out later. After that summer, though, I did not go to church again. Not for a long time.

Those gnarled branches. The alien brown hills. The winds that blew every afternoon like a gas furnace turned up too high in the winter. The unchanging climate. The continual 90 and 100 degree temperatures. The heaviness of the air at sea-level.

And the people at home. My pot-smoking landlady who stayed at her boyfriend's while her two small children wandered the street into the night. A mother who gave her kids a sandwich for dinner with the barest scraping of jelly. Her ex-husband, who leered at me every time he dropped by with a child-support check. My roommate, one of the few women graduates from the Massachusetts Institute of Technology, who became upset if I hiked ahead of her on the trail. A masculine-acting woman who had a married man sniffing after her, so she'd invite me along as protection during dark and clandestine dinners.

And the people at work. The construction workers in the cafeteria who rated the body of every woman who appeared at breakfast. Joe Wolf, another summer student, who came on to girls like a dog pissing on trees. Joe Macho, the MIT graduate student, who had never graduated in the social graces. And his roommate—Joe Motorcycle.

Joe Motorcycle and his BMW appeared to me as a knight on a white horse after a night of spaghetti and red wine, but he was just another wolf in student's clothing. He took me on a ride far up into the arid hills above Livermore one night. At a desolate scenic overlook, he informed me that I would have to put out or find my own way home. Given a choice of walking ten miles down a dirt road in the middle of the night or becoming another entry in Joe M.'s little black book, I opted for the latter.

As the nation counted down the days until its birthday, the unexplained bleeding continued. I was scared. I had to find a protector. Sex was not so much an addiction now as a bartering system. And that summer, wine was the lighter fluid.

With enough wine, I could do anything with anybody. By the fourth of July, I had already gone through three one-night stands. A boyfriend, visiting from Colorado, had driven me down the coast before dumping me on the beach in Santa Monica. And then there was that night with Joe M. None of them bought into my sex-security bargain.

Then the bleeding really got scary. One evening, as four of us were returning home on BART from an evening in San Francisco, I drenched my seat with blood. The orange woven fabric was covered with dark fluid. Looking at that mess, I hoped I had nothing to do with it. But I did. When I got home, my dress, slip and underwear were covered with blood that I could not wash out.

I wanted whatever it was to go away. Alas, the next day the drenching happened at work. Blood soaking my slacks from my crotch to my knees. Because nice girls don't bleed in public, I borrowed my roommate's midi-coat to cover my shame. A stranger gave me a ride to the local gynecologist, who performed an emergency aspiration biopsy.

Strange town, painful procedure, changing rules. It was too much.

So I drank more. Being in the land of the grape, I could buy a bottle of wine for 79 cents right there in the grocery store, next to the fruits and vegetables. Soon I was drinking half a bottle at every dinner. Big reds—those were the best. And 1976 was a great year for big reds.

Finding a protector became an obsession. Fear of more bleeding and another medical procedure fed a worsening depression. I would pay everything to anyone who would take care of me for the remaining six weeks because I wasn't functioning at all by myself.

Within two weeks of the visit to the doctor, I found him. Bob, another graduate student from MIT who liked bicycling, took me home with him one night, where I stayed the next three weeks. Now I didn't have to worry about men like Joe Motorcycle anymore, and I had someone to take care of me if the bleeding started again. In exchange, I gave Bob the only thing that I thought was worth anything—myself.

Putting out had become second nature. It was my lifeline to survival. And wine was the life raft. Wine helped numb the pain and blur my morals, With wine, I could escape into a sort of twilight zone, where the events that were happening became hazy, less real.

Those three weeks with Bob required wine. Heavy doses of big red wine. After work, we performed an evening ritual of picking up a box of macaroni and cheese and a bottle of wine. After a candlelit dinner (empty wine bottles served as candle stick holders), we'd adjourn to the bedroom.

By the time we took off our clothes, the wine was working its magic. As he pounded away, I removed myself as if I were watching a stranger perform on stage. Wine took me out of my body so that I didn't have to deal with the overwhelming consequences of my actions. It wasn't the constant risk of pregnancy that I feared the most—it was the guilt brought on by my Presbyterian upbringing. Sex before marriage was wrong, my mother always preached. If she ever found out about what I was doing, she'd never forgive me.

Although the procedure had resolved the bleeding problem by this time, I didn't hesitate to find a replacement for Bob when he returned to school. This time, Chinese food and wine purchased John, who took care of me that last week. Who cared? By this time, I had gained twenty-five pounds and lost my innocence. My self-esteem was lower than the altitude of Death Valley.

When I left California, I thought I could close the book on those twelve terrible weeks and that life would return to normal. It didn't. When I got home, Bob's farewell gift of a dozen red roses that took center stage on my parents' dining room table reminded me of my shame. Blood red roses. Big red wine. Reminders of my shame. That night, I blurted out the truth to my mother. She returned my cry for help with, "You tramp!"

After that, nothing seemed to matter. I was too far along the detour I took in California. Drinking too much at parties became a habit, as well as coming on to anyone with a deep voice and facial hair. It didn't matter that Chuck was back. I once performed oral sex with some stranger I met while Chuck waited for me outside the bedroom door. Booze lit the fire that continued to burn—the charcoals dissolving into fine, gray powder.

This is how I met my first husband a year later. Two glasses of wine at happy hour ignited a sick and troubled relationship, but by the time I woke up, it was too late. Only his desertion saved me from total disintegration.

A decade passed before I bought husband number two with two Long Island ice teas. Again, the flame of sexual desire consumed my common sense. This time, I extinguished the fire, but not before extensive damage was done.

Even now, booze and men are a combustible mixture for me. Last year, I drank beaker after beaker of rocket launchers, a mixed drink of four hard liquors. The man I ended up with that night was someone I stumbled over on the way to the bathroom.

Today, I don't trust myself. I stay away from parties and mixed drinks, from spaghetti dinners and wine—any situation that reeks of lighter fluid. Call it hiding out if you want, but I know it is the only way I can survive.

Detour

by Judith Roche

She and she and me,
we shot cocaine
all day long,
sitting crosslegged on the bed.
She and she and me,
we turned up the heat,
giggled with our child's play
and unwrapped another clean needle.
Three gone to girlhood,
circle of bruised flowers unbroken
for now, we were untouchable
in simulated second-white spilled
and mixed with pure water,
practicing for innocence
in injection of open I's.
Two of us knew our walk
on the wicked side something
borrowed to be returned
to the third, who would brunt
a burden we never bore.
I was a natural,
she said, as I found
the vein in clean thrust,
the bloody show pulled back.
She and she and me,
we all wandered
in a herd of pretty
ponies we'd dreamed
once but never owned.

Mikey's Dad

by Cindy Rosmus

For the last hour, Mikey's dad had his eye on Lisa. Mikey's dad looked like Nick Nolte, with the strangest chin—shaven, but looking unshaven and always moving, like he had to bite his tongue or he'd yell, "Don't marry him, Lisa! It's me you want, stupid bitch!"

He was too late. Father C. said the word, and then Lisa and Mikey kissed. Mikey was a rotten kisser, but he was sweet in bed. He made her feel good, talked about God and how pretty the snow was, took her to horror movie matinees. When Mikey kissed her in the church, Lisa couldn't find his tongue. That had never happened with Mikey's dad.

It was cold in the Legion hall, too Christmasy, with a shaky tree, bridesmaids in blood-red velour, the maid-of-honor in green, holly in their stiff blonde hair. Dinner would be turkey and the Veteran's Special: pigs-in-blankets. How silly to get married this day. Everyone's broke the week after Christmas. Santa's so bombed, he'd give anyone away.

Their song was "Happy," by the Stones, but they danced to "You Made Me Love You," to please Lisa's mom, the Judy Garland freak. Lisa couldn't wait for the champagne toast. She'd left her beer in the little room. The manager had practically grabbed it out of Lisa's hand when it was time to line up. ("Where's your wife, Mr. Rozewski?" the bitch had asked Mikey. Lisa was hiding in the corner. She'd held up her beer in response.) As she danced with Mikey, she watched Mikey's dad watch her. When he licked his lips, she shut her eyes.

Dancing with her own dad was like dancing with that Christmas tree. Lisa's dad was so bombed, he'd almost fallen down the icy steps of St. Jude's. He kept stepping on Lisa's gown. She remembered sitting on his lap in the corner bar, drinking ginger ale out of a whiskey glass. The glasses seemed to get smaller as Lisa got bigger. Now she drank a shot of Jack Daniels with every beer. It was Mikey's dad who'd introduced her to Jack.

While Mikey danced with his sobbing mom, Lisa sneaked a mini egg roll off a stranger's plate. He was probably a Rozewski, so she winked back at him. When she was almost through with the guy's beer, she felt someone tug on her veil. She refused to turn around, even when he did it again. "God Bless the Child" was over then. Lisa was the first to clap for Mikey and his mom. "Next one's ours," Mikey's dad whispered hoarsely into Lisa's ear.

But she got away. The toast took too long, since Mikey's cousin Zenon translated it into Polish after dragging it out in English. Lisa didn't like the soup: it was beef vegetable, with pearls of fat and canned carrot squares in it. Every time she picked up her spoon, someone started to bang his against his glass. Then they all did it.

Everyone but Mikey's dad. What was wrong with his wife? Couldn't she see through all those tears? Were they only for her late-blooming son, who still played drinking games with the Puerto Rican guys at work? Lisa looked into Mikey's eyes. They were brown and set so closely that sometimes it seemed she was all he saw, or wanted to see. She kissed him once, without the clanging of spoons on glasses. He tasted like beefy fat and warm beer.

The Veteran's band played a polka, and the old folks screamed. Lisa refused to get up. She picked at the salad while Mikey danced with the flower girl, his genius niece. Lisa looked over at Mikey's dad, but he wasn't there. Her heart jumped when she felt another tug on her veil.

"Get away from me," she muttered.

"If you want," said Mikey's dad. He sat down in Mikey's seat.

Finally she looked at him. "Go get me a beer."

He signaled the waitress instead. "Two Budweisers, please," he said in the tone of voice he used to impress young girls. The waitress was old enough to be his mother. He grabbed Lisa's hand.

"What're you, crazy?" she said.

"Maybe," he said, smiling. He looked strange in his tux. He'd trimmed his mustache and gotten a haircut for the occasion, but his hair was still too long. He and Mikey could pass for brothers, except his eyes were different: his said they were sick of seeing the same shit day after day, night after night. He put Lisa's hand on his thigh.

Lisa got up. "I'm going to puke."

Mikey's dad wouldn't let her go. "It'll pass," he said.

The polka ended, and the band announced they were taking a break. Mikey headed back to the bridal table. "The next song's ours," Mikey's dad told Lisa, "no matter what you say." He clapped his son on the back on his way to the men's room.

"Aren't you eating?" Mikey asked Lisa when the main course was served.

"I'm sick of turkey."

"So eat stuffed cabbage."

Mikey's dad kept his word. When the band came back, they started playing, "You Belong To Me." Mikey's dad held out his hand.

Lisa looked at it in horror. "No," she said.

"Go 'head, babe," Mikey said through a mouthful of food. "I'm still eating."

Lisa felt light-headed. She couldn't remember how many beers she'd had, how much champagne. She was due for a shot of Jack. She headed for the bar.

Mikey's dad seized her by the arm and led her onto the dance floor. "Later," he said. He pulled her close.

She gasped. Just once he rubbed up against her. She struggled, but there was no way out. "Enjoy it," he said.

A lot of people were dancing. Lisa saw her woozy parents, and Mikey's mom with Cousin Zen. Lisa's maid of honor was so coked up, she was trying to fast dance to the song. Once Lisa had slept with the usher her best friend was with. Tom was a great kisser, but in bed, Lisa had lost out. No one could compare with Mikey's dad.

"I'm freezing," she said.

"They just turned up the heat," Mikey's dad said.

"You're sick," she said. Again she tried to break away, but he was too strong. She saw Mikey wave to them, a glass of beer in his other hand.

"He works all day Saturday, so he'll never know," Mikey's dad said.

"Know what?"

He didn't answer. Lisa heard him snicker into her veil. They were dancing right by the bar. The bartender was grinning down at the brainy flower girl. He dropped an extra cherry into her Shirley Temple.

"He'll kill you," Lisa said.

"He'll kill you," Mikey's dad said, "if he has too much to drink. And he's pushed far enough. Then he'll explode."

Lisa could feel the little she'd eaten start to come back up. "I love him," she said weakly.

The song was ending. "Then don't tell him."

Lisa just looked at him. The other dancers clapped and stood waiting to hear what the band would play next.

She remembered the first time they did it, in the back of his van, eight o'clock on a Saturday morning. Before she ever knew he had a son her age. He had two big tattoos and a long scar around his chest, from when he was stabbed—almost sliced clean in half—in Vietnam. He'd taught her what sex was about before she even learned to drive a car. It hurt so much that she cried. Mikey's dad liked that the best. He said the more it hurt, the better it was. He said tears made him come.

Lisa was crying now, softly, on his shoulder. He smelled musky and rough, like a warrior. A chief. She let out a sob.

"Save it," Mikey's dad said.

Poppy Dreams

by Norah Philbin

The poet is drinking codeine
as if it could unstop her true voice.
Sipping and sighing
and capping the bottle.
Sighing and sipping and capping again

until her joints gel
until her head drops
until memory
gives up old ghosts
and goes quietly locking
rooms not used.

Only then does she sleep
bottle cradled between her breasts.
Her breath comes lightly as a child's
yet there is nothing of childhood
about her.

Addiction

by Sheryl St. Germain
in memory of my brother, Jay St. Germain, 1958-1981

The truth is I loved it,
the whole ritual of it,
the way he would fist up his arm, then
hold it out so trusting and bare,
the vein pushed up all blue and throbbing
and wanting to be pierced,
his opposite hand gripped tight as death
around the upper arm,

the way I would try to enter the vein,
almost parallel to the arm,
push lightly but firmly, not
too deep,
you don't want to go through
the vein, just in,
then pull back until you see
blood, then

hold the needle very still, slowly
shoot him with it.
Like that I would enter him,
slowly, slowly, very still,
don't move,
then he would let the fist out,
loosen his grip on the upper arm—

and oh, the movement of his lips
when he asked that I open my arms.
How careful,
how good he was, sliding
the needle silver and slender
so easily into me, as though
my skin and veins were made for it,
and when he had finished, pulled

it out, I would be coming
in my fingers, hands, my ear lobes
were coming, heart, thighs,
tongue, eyes and brain were coming,
thick and brilliant as the last thin match
against a homeless bitter cold.

I even loved the pin-sized bruises,
I would finger them alone in my room
like marks of passion;
by the time they turned yellow,
my dreams were full of needles.
We both took lovers who loved
this entering and being entered,
but when he brought over the
pale-faced girl so full of needle holes
he had to lay her on her back
like a corpse and stick the needle

over and over in her ankle veins
to find one that wasn't weary
of all that joy, I became sick
with it, but
you know, it still stalks my dreams,
and deaths make no difference;
there is only the body's huge wanting.

When I think of my brother
all spilled out on the floor
I say nothing to anyone.
I know what it's like to want joy
at any cost.

The Wine God's Bride

Awaiting Dionysus

by Deborah DeNicola

Ariadne awoke as the sun spilled
over the east wing of the island.
She stretched and reached for him
in the roomy bed.
But Theseus had left her,
the ball of thread
tied to her heart like a block of ice.
Stone in her throat, swollen moon
that refuses to fade with sunrise.
She swallows it over and over.
She walks the beach.

Her face in the shellshaped mirror is whiter
and thinner, more blemished,
freckled and older than she remembered.
What did he dread in her deep-set eyes?
The bleached waste of the ocean's bottom?
The low tides he would owe her?
The debt of treachery to her father
and beast of a brother?
Or was it the reckless liquor of her heights?
The mind that could slice through the labyrinth
breathing passion with manic foresight?

What did he run from?
What claws in her nest of privates?
Was it the mire of her odor after love?
Yet at times, how tender he was...
How could he simply vanish
into the halls of the horizon
leaving behind him his breath
coated with dust
like a ghost
exhaling a cigarette?

Was she to solve the mystery
that hung in the air
without a mere
goodbye? Did he tire of her
inattentive sighs, evenings, her Chopin,
the nocturne in E flat which always moved her
to pour a cognac and stare through the picture

window into the black sky—Gravity of stars
drawing her to her own thoughts.
Was it the fact that she had her thoughts?
Was it the sway and stemming of those thoughts
like the waves' repetitions that washed him away?
Or was he like her brother, a bull at heart?
Snorting for new conquests,
larger breasts, firmer ass, tighter dress—
What did he want?

Never mind. Never mind.
She stirs some tea, chops an onion, arranges
beach glass in the ash tray to catch what's left
of the morning light. The real question was
how could she hum the old warmth
in herself with a heart waning west
in its room and shrinking toward its decline?

Frozen moon. Frozen chest.
Frozen heart
only a God of Ecstasy
with a killer's rod could release

clasping and pumping the splashy
yeast of the red aorta—

Her aftershocks
like lightning in his bare hands.

Sleeping Around

by Judith Barrington

The aura of this thing is more strong than alcohol...A fine narcotic, having people in love with me   —Anne Sexton

In Figueras, Spain, where I worked from 1964 though 1966, I slept with a lot of men. Or, to be more accurate, I was sexual with a lot of men; I never actually spent a night with one. I was nineteen and terrified of getting pregnant, which I dealt with by insisting that the sex be more or less anything but straightforward penetration. There was a lot of groping and rolling around on my bed, or someone else's, with a messy, always furtive, moment of ecstasy on the part of Fernando or Francisco or Jaime, that spilled sometimes onto my bare, tanned stomach and sometimes onto the starched linen bedspread or the orange and blue beach towel. One might expect men to find this annoying, but surprising as it seems in retrospect, I always got my way.

Take for example the Italians—three of them—I met one night in Rosas. A lot of brandy blurred the events at the time as well as in my memory now, but looking back on it, I am more than a little surprised that I didn't get raped when I ended up in the back seat of a very tiny Fiat with one of them, while the other two jerked off in the front seats.

Then there was the policeman (I don't know if he was a guardia or something more elevated), I met in the small village of Gariguella at the Moli de Ven—an old windmill that had been converted into a very popular disco. All the latest American hits pounded their beat through the dusty alcoves with rickety wooden tables and candles dripping down the sides of Mateus Rosé bottles, and out into the vast night, trilling with cicadas and stars. I can still remember driving up to the Moli around the precipitous hairpin bends of the road from Perelada as "Bye Bye Miss American Pie" rolled out in wave after wave of sound across sagebrush and rock, and lizards crouched in dried-up gullies, under the star-spangled assault.

Once again, too much brandy accompanied my dancing with the policeman—dancing being an overstatement of the fact of standing up rather than sitting down during foreplay. When he took me outside and leaned me up against a Mediterranean pine, I was, as usual, compliant up to a point. When his hand went inside my underwear, I didn't object, but when he tried to replace it with his penis, I strenuously wiggled away. Spanish men, it seems, were used to this foreign standard. Without comment, he made do with my thighs and it was all over in about three minutes.

It is rather shocking to me now, looking back on all that groping, that I had no sense of my own pleasure. I was not doing it for sexual gratification—indeed I was abysmally ignorant in that area, and had only recently uttered the word, orgasm, for the first time with the woman lover I had left behind in England. My need to witness each man's desire might have marked me for a whore—albeit unpaid—had it not been for an odd kind of prudishness, which kept me from really acknowledging what was going on, even while it was going on. I didn't flirt or seduce—or if I did, I didn't do it intentionally; I merely let the sex happen and kept my dignity in the process. So what did I get out of it all? What was I looking for?

My arrival in Figueras that summer marked just six months after my parents' deaths, and I had not yet shed more than three or four tears. I had stood stoically through the church memorial service, vaguely surprised to see my sister sobbing; I had sorted the possessions in my mother and father's house, acknowledged hundreds of sympathy letters, and signed away my rights to sue the shipping line which killed my parents, all with robot-like efficiency. In spite of kind friends who tried to comfort me, I was in a world where grief nor sadness, nor any real sense of loss could touch me. Now I found myself in a new environment, intoxicated by the power of my blonde hair and long legs over all these men, distracted by the romantic notion of living alone in a small Spanish town, and anesthetized by the alcohol I used to fuel a fantasy life, which was the only life I could afford to live, The deaths hadn't yet happened in my psyche. I was aware only of a much more immediate sadness: the absence of the woman who had seduced me a couple of months earlier. That pain was as intense as the Catalan midday sun. Had I been asked, I would have said truthfully that I doubted I could survive without her.

I had created not one but two buffers against the real pain: an intense affair with a woman, doomed to secrecy and disaster, and a series of meaningless sexual encounters with men. My heart remained besieged by the first, while my body was assaulted by the second. They both worked, as any narcotic works, for a while.

When I had gone to Sofia after the funeral (she was much older and virtually a family member), I thought she would comfort me. She was the only person I knew who seemed likely to put her arms around me and talk. But something went wrong. Instead of comforting me, Sofia acted on the sexual feelings between us, diverting my huge emotional hunger into a sexual, romantic, and tragic obsession.

In Figueras, I couldn't rely on an obsession for someone a thousand miles away, even though I noted in my diary every time I wrote her a letter, or stood in line for hours trying to get a phone connection to her remote Welsh telephone exchange. My need for distraction was a daily, hourly thing. I drank, worked, danced, drove my sports car, and picked up men at every turn as if it were the only possible way of life.

I met Andres at the cafe, where I knew most of the regulars and where he came occasionally for a cognac and coffee after dinner. I knew virtually nothing about him except that he was a jeweller and that he wanted to take me around and be seen in my company. He was more than old enough to be my father, he was unattractive, and he was neither interesting nor nice to me. He was also impotent, which was about the most sexually interesting thing I encountered that whole summer. His inability to perform made me feel extremely safe, as well as more sexual than I felt with other men, and I took extremely guilty pleasure in displaying my body on his bed in the small, back street pension where he lived.

It was he who introduced me to Figueras' one and only cinema, which reeked of garlic and showed mostly cowboy movies dubbed into Spanish, viewed through a thick cloud of pungent cigarette smoke. He also took me to the theater when some traveling variety show passed through town, seizing my hand when the nearly-naked chorus girls danced across the stage and pressing it to his swelling erection which, as usual, failed to materialize later in his room. A couple of my friends from the cafe warned me against Andres, worrying, I think, more about my reputation than my physical or emotional safety. I gathered he was a bit of a rake, that he frequented the town's many brothels and that he was generally considered slightly unsavory—not because of the brothels, which surely many of the boys and men I knew patronized, but because he publicly displayed his sexual obsessions in a way that was unacceptable for a man close to sixty.

For a few weeks, however, I ignored the warnings and wandered regularly over to his pension as if in a trance. He probably thought I would employ some practiced sex tricks to turn him on, but such a thing never occurred to me, and if it had, I wouldn't have known how. I merely admired my own young body and felt sinful while he stormed around in a fury that I did not understand. When he presented me with a ring and a gold watch, I accepted the gifts, feeling like a kept woman.

The effect of my sleazy behavior was to obliterate everything but the present moment; it blotted out my longing for Sofia's arms, her voice murmuring into my receptive ear, her hands roaming my utterly responsive skin, and, beyond that, it blotted out the great and awful fact of being alone in the world before I had ever realized that such a thing could ever happen.

•••

The only men I didn't have sex with were the men who didn't try. Looking back on life in Figueras, they divide up fairly evenly into those who chose to be friends of some sort, and those with whom I had an affair. The group of boys I hung out with at the cafe in the rambla were all in the first category, except for Jose Maria, who flirted with me, but finally decided not to go that route. Arturo Suque, the handsome man who was my employer at the Perelada wine company and who was married to the daughter of the family that owned everything in Perelada, including the Castle and all its treasures, also maintained a professional distance, though I often expected and sometimes hoped for him to cross the line.

In truth, most of the flirting I did was with women—something that seemed quite acceptable in Spain, where young girls wandered arm in arm or holding hands before dinner under the elm trees around the square. I remember the intense interest, flattery, and sensuous caresses of my middle-aged hairdresser, Rosa, and the less obvious, but nevertheless intense, attraction between me and Arturo's wife, Carmen.

Carmen, the pampered daughter of one of Spain's richest families, was unlike any of the other women I had met in Figueras. She was some eight or ten years older than me and very beautiful in a fragile way. Sometimes she lived in the Castle with her three young children and a huge staff of servants, who deprived her of any tasks other than embroidery or letter-writing; at other times she migrated down to the beautiful villa on the headland at Garbet or off to the mansion in Barcelona. No matter where she was, she was lonely and bored to the point of developing imaginary symptoms for which she was sent to a Swiss heart specialist several times. When invited to visit her at the Castle, I was invariably reduced to acute shyness by the grandeur of the place and by the presence of her mother, an extremely autocratic matriarch, who made no attempt to disguise her disapproval of my appointment and her opinion that I did not belong in her drawing room. Carmen and I exchanged tentative stories about our families, but even when alone, we felt the portraits on the walls assessing our conversation. I remember her telling me about her wedding to Arturo, for which her father had knocked a hole through the six feet of solid stone that was the north wall of the dining hall and extended the long oak dining table into a marquee to accommodate a couple of hundred extra guests. Arturo, she told me, had laid down a special batch of Perelada's best red wine with a commemorative label dedicated to Queen Fabiola of Belgium, who had been the guest of honor.

One day I got a call from Carmen, who was down at the Garbet villa. It came through to the Perelada office, where I took it self-consciously in front of Ramon and Frederico, the dispatch clerks, whose communist politics led them to express grave disapproval whenever I hobnobbed with "the family." Would I like to come down tomorrow for the day? There was nobody there except her and the children, a nanny and some servants. She was going crazy, she said.

It was never really clear who was my immediate boss at Perelada. Officially, I reported to Sr. Dominguez whose office was at the shop in Figueras, so I rarely saw him, except to pick up some money now and then. But out at Perelada I operated independently, which disturbed just about everyone. Carmen's mother, for example, thought I should check out everything having to do with tours of the Castle grounds with her, or with someone connected to her household, but not her son-in-law, whose ridiculous idea it had been in the first place to hire me. The manager of the wine business, Sr. Rios, felt the same way about the visitors who trudged through the cellars, expecting me to ask him before I ushered them down the staircase into the musty chill of the underworld, with its dimly-lit catacombs, bins of dusty green bottles, and huge oak vats. But I never asked permission for anything, choosing rather to wait until someone complained. I had been asked to create my own job, and I was doing just that. So when Carmen invited me down to the coast for the day, I assumed her status in "the family" warranted my immediate acceptance without permission from anyone else.

I arrived about eleven in the morning after an exhilarating drive over the mountains and along the winding coast road. As I squealed around each hairpin bend, a new vista would open out, with what looked like a bottomless, dark green bay, almost a lagoon, enclosed within the embrace of two rocky arms on my right. To the left the hills rose abruptly, sprouting cacti and small flowers and an occasional olive grove. For the last few miles, I could see Carmen's villa, perched right on a headland, the hillside below carefully tiered and cultivated with vines. As I approached, swinging round bends, sometimes doubling back out of sight of the house, I began to pick out the terrace and the path down the cliff to a swimming pool and private harbor at the bottom.

A manservant in the familiar Perelada livery showed me though the house and out onto the terrace, where Carmen sat at a table under a shady umbrella, She didn't appear to be doing anything. After kissing me on both cheeks and pressing a cold Coke into my hand, she asked what I'd like to do. "What do you like to do when you're here?" I asked, speaking English. Her English was about as good as my Spanish, so we switched back and forth, depending on our mood.

"My favorite thing," she said, "is to take the boat out and drive to a beach that you can't arrive at by land. There are pools—what are they called, those pools where the plants grow? Ah yes, tidepools. There are many tidepools there. And then I like to fish for octopus from the boat on the way back."

"Sounds great to me," I said. "Let's do it."

After she picked up some lunch from the kitchen, she showed me to the changing rooms down by the pool, and we both set off in the motorboat wearing bikinis, with a couple of towels and shirts in case the sun got too much. I have no recollection of what we talked about, the beauty of the coast, perhaps, which at that time was still unspoiled, although further south, where the hills became softer and covered with pine trees, cheap hotels already scarred the landscape; or maybe the fish—red mullet, perch, and little sardines, which we watched from the boat as they swam along the rocks and weed which were clearly visible to the bottom. For a while we swam around, ourselves, breathing through snorkels and making faces at each other through our masks, while the anchored boat rocked very slightly on the lake-calm sea. And all day long there were silences and caresses that rarely involved physical touch, but which were passed softly from one to the other through our eyes. Just once, we put suntan lotion on each other's backs, rubbing slowly in absolute silence, both paying the most acute attention to the ever-changing place where fingertips touched skin.

When I left the villa, sunburnt and sad, Carmen kissed

me on both cheeks and said, "You must come again," but I never did. She never invited me again and I never speculated about why. I couldn't afford to examine my feelings about her.

A couple of weeks later, a young man from Perelada named Francisco, who was to pursue me ardently throughout my three years there, took me to the beach on a Sunday afternoon. "I know a beach very quiet. Pretty place too," he said, from which I deduced he knew somewhere he could make out with me in private. As he directed me to his beach, I realized we were heading straight for Garbet, and, indeed, when we came in sight of the villa, he proudly told me that it belonged to "the family." "Yes, I know," I said, rather abruptly, deciding not to tell him I had spent the day there with Carmen. Such contrasts were hard for all of us in the village, and I didn't need to emphasize my remoteness from Francisco, already being almost a foot taller than him, as well as literate, middle class, foreign, and financially independent. So there, behind a huge rock shaped like a lying-down dachshund, we embarked on a marathon session of back-rubbing (my back, his rub) interspersed with a bit of kissing and feeling around.

Nobody knew the whole story of my sleeping around. Many people knew one or two threads of it: Senor Serra knew, and disapproved of Andres; Senor Dominguez knew about my "boyfriend" Jaime, who was stationed at the military camp; the night porter at my hotel knew about Hyacinto and Jose, both of whom had sneaked upstairs with me on occasions, and pretty much everyone knew about the American boys, the waiter from Rosas, and various other dancing partners who drove in my open sports car through Perelada or Figueras in the early hours of the morning. I wasn't particularly concerned about my reputation, though I probably should have been. Somehow, my lack of concern helped legitimize my extremely unorthodox behavior and encouraged the gossips to regard me with some indulgence, since I merely laughed when they reported having seen me with someone or other in my car the night before. Had I looked guilty, I would have been crucified.

The fact was I had no guilt to spare. It was all absorbed in my obsession with Sofia. Much later I came to believe that it had been primarily her responsibility to keep our relationship on track, since I was still in shock from my parents' deaths and she was twenty years older and married to my uncle. But back then, that summer, I blamed myself. I confused the fact that I had been strongly attracted to her—had in fact had a crush on her from the first time I saw her when I was fourteen—with the fact of our now-passionate relationship. Large portions of the guilt had to do with the fact that I was acting like a lesbian (though I didn't think the actual word); the rest transformed into acute shame about my choice of her, given that my whole family disliked her, and that I was betraying them by forming such an alliance, to say nothing of the fact that it felt a lot like incest. But the secrecy she urged me to observe added to the intensity of my feelings and became an integral part of all the future relationships I would use to ward off pain.

The men weren't important enough to feel guilty about. I mostly didn't care about them, or if I did, it was a feeling quite separate from the sex. Francisco, for example, became a friend, referring to himself as my "little brother," but those relatively healthy feelings seemed pallid compared with the intensity of a brief emotional connection with Carmen or the secret yearning I carried around for Sofia. It was women I was really hooked on.

By my third year in Figueras, Sofia and I had given up trying to make it work and I was in love with another woman, Jill. I took long weekends off work and drove back to England overnight, staying up all night for three days in a row; two on the road and one with her. But I was getting very tired. The sex with men was no longer an adequate distraction; I only went on doing it to keep up heterosexual appearances, and out of habit. With women, I seemed to need more and more intensity; I got involved with someone else, while still in love with Jill, having no idea why I did it. Naturally, my inability to explain my erratic behavior compounded the guilt. Meanwhile, I became an expert at intrigue.

Although it would take years before I got to the grief—years before I learned to appreciate regular love instead of intense, guilty drama—that last summer in Figueras, I started to learn how to create periods of rest in my chaotic life—a lesson I probably learned for survival. That was the summer I discovered the rock in the river and began spending time alone there. It was a flat rock right in the middle of a fast-flowing river I found by accident one day, driving up a dirt road looking for a remote restaurant someone had told me about. I never found the restaurant, but I returned over and over to the river, sometimes taking afternoons off work with fabricated excuses, just to go and lie there like a stranded fish, with the water roaring around me and the sun burning my spray-soaked skin.

Pretty soon, my desire to go to "my rock" was almost as compelling as my overactive nightlife, but I was strangely peaceful there. I don't remember thinking about things. I just remember lying flat on my back, the rock cold and wet under my shoulders, the sky fierce and blue.

We Are Powerless

by Sallie Bingham

In New Orleans, he tells me, they laugh at the idea of spinach in Oysters Rockefeller.

Yes, I say, not really listening, being nice to get through the preliminaries fast.

This is my husband speaking and he has just come back from New Orleans where we once went together. He was looking for something or someone to fill the hole in his soul.

I have lived in that hole for eight years like a maggot, but recently I have crept out; perhaps I ate my way out through the wall of his chest.

Now he is his hole and I am no longer in it.

"Tell me about her shoes," I say. "I can tell so much from shoes."

He tries to remember, "Heels, I know. She was a lot lower when she took them off."

"Color?"

He shakes his head. "Her dress was black."

"No one wears black shoes with a black dress. Perhaps she wore red shoes."

Fragments from the stream.

Later, sitting on the bed, I tell him I no longer know how to feel jealous. Perhaps I no longer know how to feel. I am unique. The other woman is unique. All of our acts are magical.

"But if I love her?"

"Then you do."

"But I don't."

"Of course not."

"Why are you so sure?"

"Because you still have the hole."

"You don't believe love fills it."

"No. But it creates the illusion."

Later, I light a candle and watch the flame waver in the draft while he falls asleep. Later, I take his limp hand. Still later, in the dark, he howls. "Wolves were after me," he says when I wake him.

Next day I see a new bottle of mouth wash on the bathroom shelf. It is a very large bottle.

"I don't want you to drive in the evening," I say at dinner.

"You'll have to get yourself a bigger car, then. I'm not comfortable in your toilet car."

I agree.

He likes my big new car. A first when I drive he is alert, pressing his foot on the floor to slow me. After a few weeks he sits back; he begins to doze. Soon I am driving him everywhere. The mouth wash bottle empties slowly.

Coming home from work, I find him in bed with the television turned on. "I'm not comfortable. I need a new chair."

"What kind of chair?"

"An office chair. In my office I sit back and put my feet up on my desk."

Next day, I have an office chair delivered. It is upholstered in a shade to go with the rest of the bedroom. He sets it in front of a little table where he can rest his feet.

One evening while he is sitting there, I turn down the sound on the television and sing him a song. It is the one about the spider that crawls up the water spout, over and over.

He stays in bed all the next day. I make him tea.

His mother calls.

I play him music on the radio.

Next morning he gets up, exercises, shaves, dresses, reads the newspaper, and drives to his office.

He is in bed the following evening when I come home. The television is raving.

I ask him what is wrong with his new chair but he does not answer. I rub his shoulder. His face is turned away from me, towards the screen.

I pray for him and burn incense. He leans back against the pillows and closes his eyes. The mouth wash bottle is empty.

"Please start drinking where I can see you," I say the next morning.

"No. Out of respect."

"I don't need that kind of respect."

He sighs.

"I don't really mind about the other women. Perhaps they fill the hole. Just drink where I can see you."

He refuses.

They beat him as a child, but does it matter? We were all beaten, one way or another. His father lied to him; he knew, and accepted the lies. We are all lied to as children. There was a bitter ruthlessness in his father, coupled with helplessness. Does this count? His mother nagged and shrilled. What is the meaning of that? He can face an armed enemy, an earthquake, a bear on its hind legs, but not the hole.

I buy a bottle of wine and set it on the little table. He ignores it. I pour out a glass. He pretends it isn't there. Later he grows angry, insists I am criticizing him silently.

"I want to see what you do," I say.

"You see what I do. I get up, go to work, come home, go to bed."

We have not made love this season.

He sits in the new chair while I talk on the telephone. I see that the hole has burned its shape through his shirt.

"Sing with me." I touch his shoulders, his cheek, his throat. Something is stuck there—I can feel it.

That night I hold him in my arms, but now I know it is only a question of time. I can feel the heat of the hole burning into my own breast.

Mr. and Mrs. Jack Sprat

by Gianna Russo

Over the supper steaks
she asks, May I have your fat?
and he answers, Sure,
then sits and waits until
she leans back
full and satisfied,
daubing her mouth again
and again
as he empties
his full plate of food
minus two teensy bites
into the trash.
So, he's a little anorexic,
she's a little compulsive—
they find their way.
He spends Tuesday nights in therapy,
she's at Overeaters Anonymous every Wednesday
and they get by.

And some nights at two or three a.m.
when she heaves out of some dream
beside him,
he turns and sinks
his face into the hugeness
of her stomach, her breasts,
and comforted in those cushions of flesh
which fill his nose with a smell like cookie dough and
fried fish,
he knows he's completely home
while she presses her fat fingers
along his spine, his thighs,
and believes this is all
she cannot resist:
his weight, light as a child's
and his long,
lovely bones.

Party of One

by JoAnn Bren Guernsey

"You get this one," Gloria offered and edged away from the camera. "He's adorable."

"Hmmmmm," I said as we watched the man approach our counter to get his driver's license renewed. "Nice-looking enough, I guess, but kind of shaggy or furtive or something, don't you think?"

"Just your type." Gloria had been married forever and I'd just crept out from the far end of divorce like some night creature blinking in the face of the sun. Every man aged 30-50 who had most of his faculties looked, to Gloria, like my "type."

"Hello," I said to the man when he handed over his renewal form. He glanced at me, almost smiled, then seemed fascinated by something on the wall behind me.

I couldn't keep from staring at his eyebrows—so aggressively thatchy, they nearly obscured his dark eyes. They needed smoothing out and my fingers twitched. His eyes seemed worth uncovering.

"You look younger than 50," I surprised myself by saying in response to his birthdate. He did look younger, yet he didn't, as though 100 years—and not the kindest years at that—had been packaged efficiently, mercifully. I heard Gloria shuffle papers at the other end of the counter. Nobody could shuffle more meaningfully than Gloria.

He mumbled something which I didn't catch, his voice deep and musty-sounding. I wondered if it had been a long time since he'd spoken to someone.

After he'd passed the vision test, I asked him to stand on the X for his photo. Then I withdrew behind the body camera and watched him raise his bold chin toward me. His gaze steadied on the camera lens, or rather on me through the lens. A prickling sensation spread from my scalp, down my neck and kept on heading south.

"Say something," I said as I often did to loosen the mouth of whatever miserable wretch I happened to be taking a picture of. Customers usually got cute and said, "Something," or resorted to the old standard, "Cheese."

"You're so lovely you make me ache," was what he said.

Thank God I was safely hidden. I stayed behind the camera much longer than I needed to and, when I felt my face recover its normal color and temperature, I quickly handed the man his portion of the renewal form. His fingers brushed mine as he took the paper. "Thank you very much," I managed to say as a business-like way of sending him on his way.

But he didn't leave. Gloria shuffled more papers. I coughed into my hand and looked longingly at the camera for refuge.

"Want to have a drink or something after work?" he asked finally.

I nodded.

"What time can I pick you up?"

"I'm off at nine...but I'd rather meet you somewhere if that's okay."

He suggested the place, left abruptly, and I forced myself to breathe normally once again. Gloria was staring at me. To my surprise, after all the men she'd tried to drop onto me from her lofty perch as a happily married woman, all she said was, "Be careful."

His name was Sam. And it wasn't long before I discovered how uncharacteristic his first real words to me had been. In fact, he apologized repeatedly for them as though they'd been not only slightly inappropriate but insulting.

"I thought it was pretty sweet," I insisted, but that appeared to make things worse, so I added, "Let's just forget it."

We were in a quiet bar. As we sat across from one another at a table barely larger than a Frisbee, our conversation seemed to be strained through some kind of screen between us, thin enough to see through but not to touch the other side. Off and on, I could shift my focus just so, and see only the screen's mesh, leaving him an alluring blur.

"I feel about 13 years old," I admitted to him after a sigh, "on my first date ever."

"Sorry," he said. "I'm not very good at this...not good with people, I guess." His body was large but he held himself in tightly as though to appear smaller and less invasive. His hands scarcely moved as he talked, making me all the more aware of how mine fluttered and fussed with each word. Gloria's *be careful* kept clattering around in my head, and I suddenly wanted to be home in bed with a book and some Mozart. Maybe a box of Kleenex, too, just in case the book failed to entice me away from myself.

Tears were making an infuriating threat now, right in front of this quiet, oddly appealing stranger. "Just got divorced," I told him abruptly.

He nodded as though he'd guessed as much, nudged my scotch toward my hand. "It's been a while for me," he said. "But I still feel like I've left something somewhere and if I could only figure out what..."

"Well, for starters," I said, forcing a laugh, "several years have been pretty much misplaced, haven't they? And now, here I am practically middle-aged and I seem to have forgotten how to be with an attractive man."

"You think I'm attractive?"

I gave him a long look and nodded. "Of course I do. You are."

He smiled then and his face seemed to absorb every particle of light in that dim bar.

"You should smile more often," I said and then shifted uncomfortably in my chair. I was shocked to feel such moisture between my legs. If his smile could do that, what chance did I have against the proximity of his square hands, the unavoidable friction of our knees under the table?

"Let me get you another drink," he said, even though I'd barely touched the one already in front of me. I could see that what he was really saying was *Let me take care of you.*

I sipped obediently at my scotch and watched the way his

angular body moved toward the bar, then leaned against it. He started chatting with the bartender and, soon, with a few customers who sat nearby as well. I was startled, and a little hurt, by Sam's laughter and suddenly broad gestures, and by the way the other men huddled toward him. Not good with people, he'd said. Yet here, it seemed, was an instant party. Who was this guy, anyway? For a moment I played with the crazy idea of slipping away. Maybe he'd barely notice...or care.

Finally he returned with my scotch and his Coke (he'd already explained that he no longer drank anything stronger). He also carried back to me some of the mirth he'd gathered at the bar.

"Guy over there got kicked out of his house tonight." Sam squinted as he lit a cigarette. "His wife literally threw his stuff outside, right at him, including his weights."

My eyes widened. "And you were all laughing about that?"

Sam shrugged and smiled at me through his smoke. "He said she weighs about 100 pounds, his wife does, and seeing her pick up all those weights and just heaving 'em like they were sticks or something...well, I guess you had to be there to hear him tell it...."

He paused only a moment. "So...tell me how many years you've been working at that counter taking pictures and turning poor unsuspecting guys into love-sick fools."

I smiled, felt myself blush again. "Only a year and a half." What, I wondered, could I possibly mine from that job that could make for interesting conversation? In desperation, I drank faster. After all, I had two glasses in front of me which practically cried out for consumption. And he seemed more at ease somehow when I was drinking. I shut off the sound of Gloria's warning. What the hell.

His attentive eyes followed the motion of my hand as it circled the glass, raised it to my mouth, then lowered it back to the table again. I experimented a little—let the glass linger at my mouth, even discreetly licked the rim a few times. His gaze, too, lingered on my mouth. And I wondered how his mouth would feel against mine, what the texture of his chin and cheeks would be.

Before long we were giggling over nothing. Scotch can do that to willing victims. I knew (and didn't care one bit) that I'd probably acquired that goofy glazed look. And Sam had it too, in his own sober way. I found myself spilling out hoarded details of my marriage and divorce. He reciprocated with his own. We congratulated each other for surviving and celebrated with another round. His hand touched mine briefly and mine began to stroke his. When, I wondered, had ordinary, hairy, back-of-the-hand skin become so erotic?

After returning with my third drink, he leaned down to kiss me, licked his lips and said, "Hmmm. Nice." Then settled back into his chair with the grin of someone who'd just had his first taste of chocolate and was about to dive into a whole vat of it.

By now I was ready to leave with him, to be led most any-where to do most anything. Months of hunger and loneliness dropped away like a parka in spring and I felt myself open to possibilities.

But when the bar closed, so did he. In silence, we walked to our respective cars in the lot. He left me at mine with a cool kiss goodnight, and I sat for several minutes behind the wheel of my car, crying. I was appalled that I'd been so ready to go home with a complete stranger. But I couldn't quite push away the disappointment either.

He hadn't even offered to take me home even though I was clearly in no condition to drive. I found a phone booth, called a cab, and promised myself to forget him.

But I didn't.

We went out for several weeks. Usually to bars where I watched him transform himself, without alcohol, into some-one open, full of joy...sexy. More and more often, I joined the little party he could create leaning against the bar with strangers. More and more, we carried that party home with us, talking and laughing, kissing and touching. But nothing more.

Then one night I convinced him to come to my place for dinner. He brought a bottle of Chianti and, of course, scotch. I had admitted to him that I didn't particularly like scotch, but he seemed to forget. And he seldom ordered food when we were out. "You can't eat and drink at the same time," was his explanation. "Then I'll eat," I'd say. He'd look a little embarrassed and mumble something like, "Sure. I'm sorry," and watch me eat as though hunger was something more to study than to satisfy.

But at my place, with my lasagna steaming spicily on my table, I was in charge. Mozart drifted to us from the stereo, candles flickered with unseen air currents, and I was wearing a dress—a snug, thigh-length T-shirt, really—that made his eyes and hands restless. I only pretended to sip the wine he kept pouring for me. I did not want to get even remotely drunk; I wanted to feel. I wanted my mind and all my nerve endings alive and electric, because I was sure we'd be making love soon.

When we finally found ourselves in bed together, however, we seemed to need instructions. Our bodies didn't fit together quite right. Knees clashed, hands got pinned, sweat poured with effort instead of passion. He didn't want to kiss any more. Finally he just covered my body with his, rammed into me a few times and came with all the significance of a sneeze. He slipped over onto his side of the bed and we lay there in silence for several minutes.

I wanted to say or do something, maybe touch him, but I was caught in a painful limbo between laughter and tears. More than anything I felt stupid. When would I ever learn to adjust my expectations to reality? I'd lost a whole marriage, maybe even the possibility of having children, because of this defect.

Sam was fidgeting now. "Cigarette," he said and got up to pull on his pants. A few minutes later I found him sitting in my living room, staring at the full glass of scotch he'd just poured—not for me this time. I had not bothered to put clothes on. It was warm and I held a crazy hope that my nakedness might make some kind of difference to one of us.

His hand reached toward the glass, then retreated, reached again. "Five years," he said. His voice was ragged and he cleared his throat to say it again. "Five years."

I looked at his fingers edging back toward the glass. "Since you had a drink?" I asked.

He nodded. His hair was still disheveled from bed.

Oh God. Did I have to be a witness to this man's tumble

from the wagon now? "That's a long time," I said lamely.

"Not after 30 years of being a drunk, it isn't. I had this way of living, you know? It came in a bottle, and when I emptied one, I could buy or borrow or steal or whatever another one." He paused, gave me a look that said I was from another planet so why even bother talking to me, then dropped his gaze back to the shimmering glass.

"It was like giving up a limb," he added under his breath.

I wrapped my arms tightly around my ribcage and took a deep breath. "That took a lot of strength," I said. "A lot of courage."

"Strength?" He snorted and glared at me. "Courage? Are you kidding? Give it up, lady. Don't make me into some kind of goddamned hero just so you can find something to care about. That's for you, not me. There's nothing here."

"Nothing at all?" I unfolded my arms, stepped toward him.

He finally let his eyes take in my nakedness, but looked away, annoyed, and shook his head.

The drink sat untouched as he slumped back in the chair. I could almost feel the numbness in him seep into me as well, maybe the only kind of seduction he knew. It had a certain appeal to me too—no feelings, no pain, no fear.

But I went to him instead, knelt on the floor between his knees. "Sam." As I pulled myself up and leaned into him, my breasts stirred the hairs on his stomach. I dotted his chest, his neck, and then the rugged terrain of his face with the softest of kisses until, after pausing a moment, my mouth dipped into his.

A low, muted "uh" came from somewhere in his throat and his hands began stroking up and down from the small of my back.

"Now we can make love," I said.

His hands stopped cold in their journey. "That word," he said hopelessly.

I pulled back just enough to see the blankness in his eyes, to put my own reflection there. "What word? Love? You don't like it? Tough. It's what we're going to make."

"Don't think so," he said, but I didn't listen. And we did.

A tangle of hours later, when we finally fell asleep, it was with the weight of his arm still holding me in place.

But the next morning, he was gone. He left the scotch still untouched, but that was all. Naturally, I looked for a note—romantic or regretful or whatever. Nothing. So I wasted no further time before ripping sheets from the bed, tossing out cigarette butts, washing dishes, opening windows. In the shower I could find relief from his scent, his touch and taste. Besides, the shower was the best place to cry and hardly notice.

But it was not so easy to wash away the bitter questions. What could I have done differently? What more? I asked and ached until, finally, the answer came. Nothing more. And to the inevitable question, about what had I expected, I found a quiet new answer—an awe really, of myself and of others. What to expect? *Everything*.

I saw Sam a few months later when I was waiting, with a date, for a table in a restaurant. He was leaning against the bar sipping his Coke, gesturing broadly and laughing. Sam and three other men held their cigarettes, their glasses, and their stories with the careless generosity of strangers. His smile created a light in the hazy cube he occupied with the others who grasped for his words like party streamers pinned to smoke.

Bones of Lovers

by Madelyn Camrud

I've never truly let them go,
those lovers who drained my blood
the way cancer claims a victim,
until a body, cell by cell,
breaks down. That last January ghost
hasn't left me; I can look at his teeth
and see bones, wet and gleaming.
He's taken only the gift I painted him:
White gulls in flight, a clear sky
with some words about spirits, underneath;
a framed transfusion for him who left
me dying. I knew what empty was then;

now it's returned, another season:
the lovers I can't deny, grand, roving;
they should have gone to their graves
long ago. Their letters and phone calls
never convinced me I was desirable,
not then, not today: loveless lovers
inside me still whisper of meetings
in hotels as if my body were only
for devouring. Why can't they die

and let me live? Never having known love
in the way I wanted, always failing
to satisfy their longings and mine,
I live with the agony of bones, growing
restless inside of me. It's July,
yet a blizzard of white faces swims
in my head; their cries drifting,
swelling to moans till my brain
freezes over: those lovers grope
for an opening in the darkness,
tapping the walls of a body that echoes
and closes, too cold to let them go.

Stuffed On Empty

by Marti ZuckroV

A long time ago there lived a woman who ran after people so she could swallow their troubles. In the beginning she was fast, like the cheetah. She would gobble up a lost child, a broken dream in a flash; "gulp" and it was gone, sliding down her throat, liquid.

She nourished herself on their disappointments, a wounded heart, a hand no longer held, an empty cupboard. She knew her city very well. The nooks and crannies where young lovers fought among themselves, where old men lived alone and old women cooked for no one, feasts turning rancid as their hair turned gray. She would overeat then, slowing down while she hunted for more, so insatiable was her need to take away their pain.

On desperate days, strangers would suffice. She would track them down, her long legs stretching the length to their secret grief. Theirs wasn't as tasty, but it would do until a huge, juicy tear in someone's heart close to her called to her like a magnet. She would swallow it whole then, licking her lips. These were her favorite meals, a son, a daughter, a lover, a husband, a close friend's despair.

She grew fat. Her once lithe body weighted down. Her belly swollen, bursting through the cloth that covered her arsenal of pain, not hers to vomit up, making room for another binge of someone else's heartache. She stalked at night then in the quiet hours. When she, like a beggar, hid behind troubling nightmares, restoring peace to the flickering eyelids of those lucky enough to find sleep one more time. She lifted their pain with the skill of a surgeon, her expertise magnificent.

After years of gorging herself on the hardships of everyone she knew, the woman became so fat that she could no longer walk though the front door to leave her house. Her face, once round and beautiful, was now red and swollen. Like the sores of a leper, the woes of the world ate at her flesh.

People came to her then, slipping their lost love affairs under the door, pushing a broken promise through an open window, leaving a disappointment in her mailbox. She ate mercilessly now, afraid it might be her last drop of nourishment, stuffing the wounds into her mouth, sucking them dry.

One day she tried to get up from her bed. Her legs could no longer hold her body up. She collapsed back onto the mattress. Her huge frame shook, flesh rolling like a waterfall. Terrified of the famine she now faced, she held her breath till she could no longer stand it, then sobbed herself to sleep. She woke the next morning feeling a ravenous curse throughout her enormous body, desperate to chew on another's hurt in order to feed the hole inside her that now grew wider by the minute.

Days passed and her hunger grew louder and louder as she lay trapped in her body. She was starving for someone else's grief, thirsting for someone else's misfortune. If she didn't take another's pain away soon, surely she would die. She tried her right hand first. Pushing her stubby fingers into her mouth she quickly devoured all but the bones. Next her arm, then a shoulder.

The morning found her there, graceful and still, lost in the emptiness she held. No longer stuffed with their misery, she felt herself for the first time. She felt herself in the room, in her bones, in her heart which now belonged to her. Like an infant she explored the newness of herself, amazed with each discovery of her being. Her own pain was marvelous, like traveling to an uninhabited galaxy. She stepped slowly, cautiously, wondering, taking in each morsel of herself. Her loneliness was salty, her grief tender. She ate slowly, tasting each year for its vintage, sipping her life. No longer a woman driven into the streets, she hunted no one. Her days were spent in thought, her nights in dream.

On a spring afternoon, many years later, her bones gave out. She had grown old and brittle. She lay down for her final sleep. Her arms turned to dust, her legs became powder, her skull crystal. Her heart opened, drawing a bright red circle around her once human body.

Needless to Say

by Mary Ann Schaefer

Take this body, for example, it's been
the rounds with no qualms for twos
or threes or being tied down to that
which I could never contain. Take these

breasts for another, with a forward jest
and malice of forethought, like
candy, it's said, sweet and chewy
like candy. Take my cunt if you must

call it that, with the pride of a down
and out tongue; it gives you the right
of way, yielding me blood brazen hussy
sleaze dirt bike street dyke and

give it to me again good. Take
what you please—for god's sake just
take it or leave it without a word or
any cry of protest from me, the unsinkable

stranger, the consenting adult who sleeps
in Southern Comfort fumes and only
occasional cottonmouth tremens. And I
concede it all, been there more times than

I've cared. The shame tastes like burnt
toast, like becoming what I never wanted
to be in the face of all my woman-ideas lying
crushed on the rocks, only to surface gasping gentle

gentle touch my gentle desire soft want warm
nymph dream, remember our name, and take
my breath away at just the
given moment

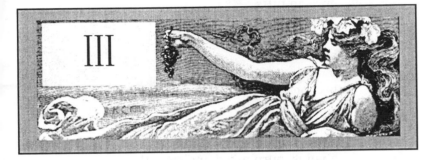

The Dance of
Addiction

Dancing with Pan

by Alison Luterman

Watch
out for him, I warn you,
with his furred hind-
quarters and coiled
goat's tail like a hairy
arrow, pointing
somewhere ambiguous. Black
hair
curls in tufts
around his ears;
a white-toothed grin
and long
musician's fingers
beckon.
      Watch
by the magic pool,
he'll come, his curved
phallus, purple-red and smooth
as a horn of plenty, his
sloe-eyed opening request
of you to dance just once
and you do,
knowing better
and all the while
music plays and the
carefully planned and
planted garden you had
thought you wanted
for your life (your
life) tilts
and slides: Private
entrance, sundial,
ornamental shrubs—the whole
shooting match—into
the reflecting pool.

Blue

by Marnie Maguire

The person I have loved the most had nicks in his fingers, chunks missing at the joints. Oil and blood had sunk permanently down to the moon of his nails. All day he stuck his hands into the fat mouths of automobiles and took them out in the evening, eaten alive by the engines. On the way home, he'd grow angrier and his hands would sprout like barbed wire and jagged stumps from his shirt sleeves, until he was home with two live monsters swinging from the ends of his arms. He was my first lover. It was mother who taught me to mix this ugliness in my heart. It was my mother who taught me to mix my love with fear.

Now, I hide from them beneath strangers' bed sheets.

I say to the stranger at the bar,

> *Will you be my lover?*
> *Will you let me press my blue lips on you?*
> *Will you feel the shock of my love in your groin?*

I circle him in candles.

I check his fingers for nicks and blood.

I check his mouth for my mother.

I stare hard at my hands and crawl into his bed, move through the night, listening for the snap of bone, the moist bite of teeth, the whip of a skipping rope.

In the morning I leave without a mark and walk. I tell myself to keep going. Don't stop. Keep going, and the rain starts down and pins me slowly to the sidewalk. I keep walking, waiting for the pain, expecting to be pushed hard to the ground, my throat to be slit, a knife in my heart. I wait for it. But while I wait I can feel the pain. I feel it as if it were real—

the sharpness of it. I feel wrapped in blood.

I have walked through three towns, seven parking lots, five fields, two highways, one river and a shopping mall. My feet grind on the pebbles and pavement. My back folds in the dips of the streets. I can feel the night returning across the sky, and I am thinking, I have not found a sheet to hide beneath.

I pass a bar and see lights moving inside. I hear the clink of glass and voices. The shadows of bodies move behind the window, and I know I can take one, lead it back to its bed where I can hide again tonight, rising up and down beneath the sheets.

But I tell myself to keep walking. I am still feeling unmarked from the last night and all the others. And it is no use. I don't want to crawl beneath another body, hide beneath another sheet, blind my eyes in another dim shadow of a bar. I want the cold of the night pressed against my face. I want to press my luck with the muggers, the murderers, the people with the guns. I want a small gash or a slit or a hole, as if then my skin will open up and say, ahhh, let go of this pain.

I need to go home. Back to my friends, Cara and Alisa. Or to a house of mirrors. A place of glass. A place where I can watch myself, see my sleep coming and stop it. Because with it comes—they're there—my mother and lover waiting for me in the center of my sleep.

I walk all the way back to the antique shop on Queen Street. I stare at the naked mannequin behind the glass with her face half gone and scream up for Cara. She dips out from the window. She smiles and lets the keys fall through the air into the cup of my hands. It hurts.

"You've been gone so long," she says.

• • •

We are sitting in the dark drinking bowls of beet red wine and eating gold strings of pasta that Alisa has spun in the kitchen like a silent weaver. Alisa's plants hang dark green and dry like long stemmed roses from the ceiling. She smokes her pot. There is a glaze and a grin over her dough face that sinks and rises as she smokes.

Cara's lips are wet as they always are, and she moves them up and down like two small dancers and says, "Where have you been this time? In the bars? With the strangers? You can't hide. You shouldn't have left. The night is hard for me, too."

"I know," I say.

"Alisa sleeps all night," she says, "I've needed you here."

"I'm sorry," I say.

Cara smiles, swallows her wine and pours us all more. We drink it and become silent for a moment, then speak in slow moving gestures. I am fallen back on a cushion. I am stuffed with the bread and oily olives and whipped cheeses and gold pastas that Alisa has offered. My cheeks are flushed from darkness and candles and wine and I have Alisa's stoned hand on my stomach, kneading her fingers softly upward to the rhythm of Cara's dancing syllables that have broken the silence and are falling from her wet mouth, curving up and around my ears.

"Don't leave us again," she says.

We fall asleep; the fire is burning the house down, the candles turning to liquid dribble, dripping down the banister, into the antique shop, blending the naked mannequin with rose wax and smoke. We all turn into flaming marigolds.

And then to naked, wet birds in a delicately strung nest. My beak is wide open, "Are you my mother?" My mother nods her head. Brings out her machete from her perfect little purse and chops off half my head.

Cara shakes me, says, "You have to find your hands."

Between us, Alisa sleeps loudly. I remember now that she has always done this. Cara and I try to stop her. Cara sticks her finger in Alisa's mouth. I lean on her nose, clogging it with an elbow, but the snores burst from her ears like grass and we roll off the bed, into another dream.

Cara wraps my rubber band around my throat, takes my tiny blue bottle of heroin and slides the shock of my needle into my vein, flaring up like a light from my neck. My blue drug trickles in. My skin goes, ahhh.

"I feel better now," I say.

We draw pictures of our hands.

"If you look at your hands before you go to bed," Cara says, "you will be able to control your dreams."

"And if this doesn't work, walk to a mirror in your sleep," I say.

"This is like déjà vu," she says. We've had this dream many times. The hands and the mirror and the blue drug. It was the first, the second or the third dream that we spoke in front of the hospital late at night, her white cast glowing between us. The next thing she said to me was, "My boyfriend says, I am the perfect Bozo doll." and I knew what she meant. I said, "See these. These blue marks on my neck. My boyfriend held me in the air like a bell by the throat just this evening." And we both burst out laughing. "Ding Dong." I said. "Ring-a-ling-a-ling," she said.

"Was that the alarm?" I ask.

"No, it is not morning yet. Oh, the night," Cara says.

"Please pin me more blue," I say.

Cara squeezes my neck, gets the needle and sticks it in.

She says, "There are bullets where my eyes should be and I am afraid that they'll turn inward in the night."

"But if you look at your hands..." I say.

"If I look at my hands one more time," she says, "they will scratch out my eyes."

"In the last dream," I say, "I flew to the mirror to save myself, but I was covered in blood and there were blue bruises on my neck the shape of giant rain drops."

"If I shall die before I am broken," she says.

"I pray the Lord my soul to break," I say.

• • •

"Alisa," we whisper, "We need to eat."

We lift her limp body from the bed and take her like the dead to the Kensington Kitchen where we are surrounded by wood and tapestry and drooping snapdragons.

We are eating sugared pancakes and hot cocoa in the restaurant because it soothes my blue drug when I get too cold. Alisa is moaning about the food. Her face is rising and sinking. She is smoking a joint in the restaurant between bites as gigantic as my heart.

Blue stars are bursting in my blood. Cara is speaking with

exclamation marks, I stare at her stained lips and see that there are beet red bubbles spewing out so quickly, bursting beside my eyes and ears. Stars are bursting everywhere in my body and my mind. I cannot eat for all the explosions. I sit at the corner of the table and cry all over the pink cloth.

Cara holds me in a toilet stall. Her stained lips on my forehead. I can smell her perfect cream neck, the smell of sandalwood. I can see the wine running right below her skin. We take out her red lipstick and scrawl hearts and hammers and stones and arrows and LOVE! all over the bathroom walls.

A woman from the real world walks in holding her purse, her head, her mouth as if everything in her world is perfectly composed. The red frightens her and she backs away from the toilets and us as if we are holding a sharp, shiny knife to her throat.

"I am cold," Cara says. "Not just cold. But freezing. Ice. Cold."

"It is because we are not really in a restaurant," I tell her. "We are in an igloo."

See the igloos we have made of ice? See the pretty blood we have painted on the walls with the pretty seal that walked in on our ritual? See how we have sliced her open for her pretty heart?

See our love?
See what my mother has taught me?
See what my lover has taught me?
See?

"Look at your hands!" Alisa screams. "Look at your hands!" Alisa screams, "Look at your hands!"

"She is so loud," Cara says.

"Yes," I say, "Pin me more blue, will you please?"

● ● ●

Alisa leads us back home. She curls herself onto a cushion and sleeps. Cara and I stand by the window.

"You are completely blue," she says. "It's like an aura all around you. I have never seen anything like it."

I smile. "It is almost over," I say, "The night."

"Yes," Cara says. We rest our hands on each other's and watch the night leave. The one speck outside the window. The last star on the black olive morning and the silhouettes of mist and the clouds like black blue bruises on the fleshy, swollen sky that surrounds our window and pushes against the pane.

Used To

by Cheryl Townsend

Shoot 151 like milk
take men like vitamins
never gave out my
phone number never
brought them home
kept score until it
got too boring
would dance dance
dance til the bars
closed down then
dance some more
on a cock telling
them I never had
the same hangover
twice either

Codeine Poems

by Anne F. Walker

1
Both eyes full
of black.
A cough-syrup-sweet blank
dances quietly into a mirror.
His syringe on the floor.

2
Drowns like

it's like a strangle hold
over your chest.

You are lying in a deep blue
a wave of cold passes over you
stains your bones blue
  under loose skin
still holds

a strangle knot
    blue veins,
the man with sunken blue eyes
throws you an artery ladder,
your hands can't grasp
(veins were yours)
in your hand no longer moves,

Flesh dead cold.

3
It's after late
inside, my body hot
so much numb coated over my tongue.

I hear a knock at the third story window.
I am afraid.
This is a cold frightening place.
     Early dreams
               move so quickly
          friction burn wakes me.

A thousand tired hands
could touch me now
and the violent possessive passion would still be dead
     buried under tears and words
and time and pain unexpressed.

4
Her voice gets smaller
each time she says she loves him.

Curled up closed
their skins are the same color.
She touches for last breath.

You reach around my legs
wrap them in your arms.
You have such long arms.
My body in an S to yours.
Head tucked behind neck.
His and hers.

Going Out for Cigarettes

by Lisa Horton Zimmerman

Clarisse was sitting on the couch painting her toenails a deep orange color. She could get away with this with her dark hair and olive skin. Jimmy was watching a Reds game on their small t.v. Once in a while he'd stand up and blow a loud, shrill whistle between his thumb and forefinger. This might mean he was happy with the game, or not. Clarisse was never sure since she didn't watch baseball with him. It sounded like a good whistle to call a dog, a big dog.

"Jimmy," she said, looking over at his thin, tan body slumped down in the blue easy chair. "Hon, I feel like going out to a bar and smoking cigarettes."

"You quit, Clarisse. Remember?"

She leaned over her feet, which were propped up on the coffee table, and blew lightly on her toes. "Well, we could go and just have one beer and one cigarette." She knew when she said it that if they did go they might have more than one drink and one cigarette, but she liked feeling that maybe they wouldn't. Maybe they'd be good and come right home after sipping a cold beer, really slow, and watching Clarisse blow tiny smoke rings into the air.

"Come over here and sit on my lap," Jimmy said, during a commercial.

Clarisse walked gingerly across the carpet to Jimmy's chair and sat across his thighs.

"They look pretty," Jimmy said, looking down at Clarisse's toes. "Like little mandarin oranges." He kissed the bruise on her upper arm. "Mike says we've got some work next week."

"What kind?" Clarisse asked, watching a woman doing aerobics, advertising some special kind of shoes. Or maybe it was her outfit which was sleek and shimmery.

"Dry wall."

"Okay," Clarisse said. "Let's go out for just a little bit. And celebrate." She looked out the living room window. The afternoon sunlight was weak and watery. She felt suddenly afraid.

"You cold, baby?" Jimmy asked, hugging her to him, a little bit too tightly. She tried not to squirm, took a small deep breath instead.

"Can't we get a dog?" she asked.

"But then you get work, what'll we do with the dog?"

"It's hard when you're gone."

"Let's go out," he said. "This game sucks anyway. And you're so pretty I could eat you one little bit at a time." He smacked her lightly on the rear when she got up.

They walked to the bar on the corner. There was nowhere else. Not nearby. They'd sold their car. But she'd lost her license anyway. An open bottle in the car, what did she expect? Jimmy was calm but firm about this. He told her she was no teenager.

Of course Mike was in the bar. He bought Jimmy a shot of something, and Clarisse went to the vending machine and bought a pack of Kools. It had been a week since she'd had a cigarette. They cost so much money. The machine ate her quarters slowly, as if they were delicious.

She got matches from the bartender, and when she sat down Jimmy asked why she wore so much mascara.

"Because you like it."

"Whatever you say."

Clarisse blew a big smoke-ring and then a smaller one through the middle of it. She loved the taste of menthol.

"Your dad was too easy on you when you were little," Jimmy said out of nowhere.

"My dad cut down a whole row of lilac bushes because my mother loved them," Clarisse said.

"Sounds a bit too perfect to be true."

Clarisse's face felt warm for a second. "What do you mean

by that?"

"Sounds like a story, honey, that's all." He smiled across the table at her, then raised two fingers up to the bartender.

He has such beautiful bone structure, Clarisse thought. He had a carved face, like polished wood. She drained her glass.

"You can't smoke this whole pack, now," he said, tilting his head, like a school teacher might, and sliding the pack of cigarettes next to his glass. "You ask me when you want another, okay?"

She wanted another cigarette instantly, but thought of other things. She was adept at thinking of other things during an unpleasant experience.

Mike came over with a tray of shot glasses filled with something minty. Not the ordinary Schnapps.

"Hmm, wintergreen," Jimmy said, sniffing.

"This stuff's great. Hundred proof. One for the lady?" He looked at Jimmy when he asked. Jimmy looked at Clarisse, and Clarisse smiled sweetly and shrugged. Sometimes her heart beat so quickly she thought she should see a doctor. But it wasn't all the time.

"Sure," Jimmy said, sliding the pack of cigarettes back across the table. "Next one's on me." He winked at Clarisse, and she felt his hand lie down on her bare thigh like a warm, live thing, something other than a hand.

It was dark when they walked home. Jimmy was reaching up under her shirt. He liked to undo parts of her clothing before they got inside. When he stood up from the table she'd put the Kools in her purse. She could go out on the little porch and have a cigarette afterward, when Jimmy slept with his arm thrown up over his head, as if he were waving to someone far away. She would sit out there under the cracked glass stars and think about the dog they'd get from the city pound, how big he would grow, and how ferocious and quiet he would be whenever she was alone, or afraid.

Not Quite Gunpowder

by Jackie Sheeler

we rode these streets
in your loaded yellow Oldsmobile
or my beat-up old black one, and swore
through the grey glaze of a thousand
over-processed poppies, that
we sure were something special, swore
that nothing and no one could ever touch us.
after the feds took one car and one
careless nod took the other,
we walked these streets,
not so untouchable now.
we put up fronts, like a shopkeeper
barricading his windows against the looters in a mad riot.
sheets of steel, lots of nails, anything
to cover up the possible and lock out the chances
of going down, and away from one another.
we staggered back to the apartment we soon would lose,
loaded down with the deadweight of countless
empty bags and a tired pair of strangling hearts.
who choked those hearts except for us?
did each one die a little bit
every time we tied off for a hit?
or does it happen all at once, like
a nuclear reactor creeping up to a critical mass
atom by slow atom until the last molecule glows red
and the whole damn mess blows straight to hell?
for me, for now, the riot is over and the reactor is cold.
but i still can feel a sniper waiting out there,

somewhere, with a rifle aimed straight at your neck.
his weapon is loaded with sets of works
and his ammunition is not quite gunpowder
but something definitely lethal and infinitely slow:
if the wound doesn't kill, the infection will,
and I'm not going back on that battlefield:
> not for you, or love of you, or missing you,
> because the sniper's sights are trained and ready
> and he just might have a shot for me.

Old Records

by Elspeth Cameron Ritchie

A lonely night—time to take care of some long procrastinated tasks like throwing out the old scratchy albums and my ex husband's overalls, and transcribing my dough- and wine-stained address book.

First the records. They clog my shelves, and, showing their sleeves, tumbling like overweight women out of their jackets. I've been meaning to toss them for ages. Since the start of my new life, I play tapes instead. I've been resisting buying CDs, so that I wouldn't declare my past completely obsolete.

It's hard though. These albums date back twenty years (am I that old?). My first purchase, age fourteen and teenybopper, was Jimmy Cliff's *Give Thanks*. I hadn't heard of him, but liked the album cover. Bruce Springsteen's Sandy—how can I discard that memory? My first boyfriend, Jim, and I listened to it as we drank Pink Ladies, gin and pink lemonade in my bedroom. (The bong was hidden behind the speakers, but I am sure my mother smelled it.)

Jim left me for my best friend two weeks later. Two years later, after many more girlfriends, he shot himself. I remember him whenever I hear Bruce wailing.

So many of those early records were tied up with rebellion and drugs, like Alice Cooper's I'm Eighteen, which we chanted through our graduation year, even at my private girls' school. Steppenwolf boomed "Born to Be Wild" at high school keg parties. For most of us, our revolt was limited; we ended up at good colleges and are now doctors, lawyers, bankers.

As I continue to dig through the pile, I find records belonging to old college roommates, sweet memories of Bonnie

Raitt in *Streetlights*. I played it while making out with my roommate's boyfriend; she never forgave me for that. I met my husband, Dick, to *Turning Japanese*, in retrospect a bad sign.

Next medical school, driving in at 5:30 a.m. while the radio belted the Talking Heads' *Take Me to the River*. I would hum it while holding human hearts in the operating rooms. I loved to dance to the Heads, but didn't like dancing with my fiancé—he would get too drunk and his arms flail up and down, looking ridiculous. Another bad omen—why didn't I pay attention?

Dick and I eventually got married. The stereo system was a composite of both our equipment. A good couple of years, but his dancing never got better, and the drinking got worse. We slipped together into alcohol, and along with it, not talking about what really mattered.

Another man came along as the marriage decayed. Temporarily it was Brahms on the radio and his CDs, and sobriety. I never bought any classical records though. And I never slept with him. Still, Dick was jealous. Ironic that those sweet musical notes helped end a marriage.

Because of my next passion, I switched to buying tapes of country music, and listening to Reba McEntire and Doug Stone, while drinking vast quantities of beer with the boys. Such good words to get drunk to; it seemed condoned by the musicians wailing about love and loss and whiskey.

The record buying ended soon after, along with my marriage. After the divorce I kept my ex-husband's broken turntable and mammoth speakers. He exited with most of the new albums, mainly New Age. I held onto Kim Carnes, *I Miss You Tonight,* a very worn disc, but I still play it when I lie sleepless, regretting my past mistakes. I can't get rid of that one.

The marriage is over. Dick is gone, living with another woman. Yet the habits of drinking and smoking I picked up with him persist. His girlfriend (wife now?) made him quit cigarettes. I should have done that, before I got started, or developed a taste for scotch.

I now love the strong lyrics of Tracy Chapman and Marie Chapin Carpenter ("sometimes you're the windshield, sometimes you're the bug, sometimes it all comes together, some-times you're just a fool in love"). Unable to completely cut loose from the tune of my past, I box the old records and store them in the guest bedroom. One of these days, I will get around to throwing them out, as well as revising my address book. Right now, I recognize it is more important for me to break free of the alcohol and nicotine addiction I have carried away from this divorce and that now clogs my life.

Wynona Judd plays "Love is Alive." If I can make the space for it, I hope it *will* be for me again.

Just like Sister Ray Said

by Alison Stone

When I'm scared in New York City
All the buildings look like hypodermic needles.

I am like a child looking through a peephole
In a piece of cardboard.
I bump into things and nurse my bruises through the dawn.

My only childhood toys were red balloons
Marked "gambling," "overeating," "drugs."
I am not angry
My parents could not give me
More than they had.

At twelve starvation was the answer.
I would appease God by becoming Him on earth.

When my fourteenth detox failed
I thought of my father
Choosing his daily rations
From the vials of brightly colored pills.
No one can accuse me of disloyalty.

After a certain point
The reasons no longer matter.
My tracks are paths
Leading away from what is really wrong.
A hermaphrodite, I revel in self penetration
And avoid the messy question of sex.

Nothing can keep me free
From the false self which makes my body hard to bear.
My skin is missing layers, my fingernails are too big,
My teeth are overcrowded in my mouth.
Everything I am is magnified.
My sensations swallow the world until I am the world.

Reefer Sadness

by Gwendolyn Bikis

In just a few more days, I'll be seeing Tammy. Kissing her lips, her nose, her softly pulsing throat. Holding again her gaze, darkly, warmly drawing me in, and down, wrapping my arms and legs and whole self all around her again. And then we'll be able to talk again as though trust were actually a tenet of our relationship.

In just a few more days I'll be on a bus toward North Carolina, and I'll be seeing Tammy. The happiness, the eagerness I feel has gotten me out of bed every morning, has given me the motivation to maybe get my life straight.

Now that I've cleaned and straightened this room, now that I've filled out a couple of job applications, now that I have called Tammy and written her, there is only one thing I have to do in order for my life to feel nice and neat again; I need to smoke some marijuana. *Dope,* I used to call it before Gloria, my prison mother, corrected me—"Don't be callin' it after King Heroin. Dope is dope." "There ain't no hope with dope," added Thelma, displaying her battle-scarred neck and calves and thighs and arms. *Reefer,* I've since learned to call it; pot, my mother called it; herb, the black people in Baltimore called it; grass, Paul called it. Weed, Rodney and Buddy used to call it in college. Rodney and Buddy, their eyes swollen slits while they gorged on butter-laden biscuits and bowl after bowl of ice cream at Saturday-night supper. "We got aholt to some reyudbud," Rodney would whisper, his drawl more soft and sibilant under the influence. "Well, where'd it go to?" I asked, having that morning been promised some. "Up in smoke," he giggled.

Sweeter than dreams, stronger than prayer, faster than aspirin, more reliable than any lover: reefer. This morning, when I awoke, a ray of hope fell across my bedspread, and I wanted to really feel it in order to believe it; and I couldn't unless I was high. I spent the whole day yesterday leafletting for Lingua Franca, and I knew, as soon as they laid the 40 dollars cash in my palm for ten hours' work, what it was I would spend at least some of it on. I'd take my chances with lurking undercover narcs if I could have my high again.

Reefer got me over; over my family—I could sit in my room stoned, listen to my radio, and manage to ignore my father's sodden snoring, my mother pounding the headboard, the sex and shouts and crying that went on in my parents' room next door. Reefer got me over high school—I could buy a nickel bag and unroll the joints inside, stuffing weed into my Salem 100's and smoke it at the boulders on the edge of campus that every head knew well and the administrators ignored, and go on to Social Studies and pretend it was enrapturing and get an A on the essay test. Reefer got me over prison—I could score some in the far, dark corner of the gym that every inmate knew and every guard ignored, and smoke it in the shower in the five-minute confusion between Watch Shifts, and bounce out to the rec yard, lean against a sun-bathed brick wall, and groove, just as though the fear and rage and boredom all around me were not anything I felt inside. Reefer set me free.

Yesterday, after I got paid, I came back here and sorted through my change: I had four extra dollars, even after phone calls to Tammy. I could spend some money on reefer and not even have to feel guilty. I fished a five dollar bill out of my pants pocket, stuffed it into my jacket pocket, stashed the rest of my money away, and headed for the park where I scored.

The reefer will help me write, I think, as I stuff a towel along the bottom crack of the door and unroll the bag of seedy, stemmy weed that smells like pencil shavings. "Street weed," they called it in prison, and some of the less desperate claimed they could wait till something better came in. "That shit ain't shit," Gloria would sneer, "I don't make but two bucks a day, grade three work, so you know I ain't gonna lay nothing out for that kind of shit weed," "You want a toke?" I'd teasingly offered my burning joint. Her nostrils had flared. "Yeh." Well, that sure got your nose open, I thought as I watched her suck the joint with her eyes closed. "Aaah," she exhaled, deeply contented. Reefer had been sent to us, the state-punished, by the vagaries of a merciful God.

I open my window and glance around my room, taking stock: bare walls, stained ceiling, a sink that drips. In front of me, the water-warped records I rescued from Ralphie's basement. Every time I see my ruined Stylistics record, the one with "You Are Everything," my favorite song when Tammy and I were flirting or courting or doing whatever we were calling it during college—every time I lay my eyes on that utterly ruined record, I get so mad my throat burns. I light my joint.

Aaah...my head swells with warm euphoria. I breathe more smoke down: a weight lifts, for the first time since I've been out of prison —I really was in—I take another toke—but it's all over now. Everything that happens, happens for a reason. It's a thought I'd never have, much less believe, if I weren't high.

Besides, prison wasn't always that bad. (When I'm high, I can even, somehow, convince myself my family wasn't that bad.) The boredom. the every day after every day after every day that somehow plodded past, would waste away when I was high. Walls would fall, ceilings disappear; mesh and fence would melt. With boredom as its base, my mind could fly. And in prison, I was tighter with my pals than I'd even been in high school, and, except sometimes for Rod and Tammy, than I'd ever been in college.

"My ship done come in," Gloria would whisper to me at noon feeding. It meant that we would meet in the shower, as soon as the morning guard left and the new one—the one too weary and sloppy to want to notice—came on. Gloria always got good weed, and she always shared it with me; and we'd hang out stoned in a corner of the yard with her radio and talk about ourselves. Under the influence, I probably told her more than I ever told anyone, Tammy included. Gloria was so honest about her life that I couldn't feel embarrassed or ashamed for myself for long.

"Soon as I seen you come into this Ward Unit, I said to

myself, this little baby's in for some hard, hard time. Sweet meat, we used to call your kind around my way. Because I know how people get when they see someone so little and ...white. They get vulturous. But when I seen you with that strut—where'd she get that at? I thought. (The Dap we used to call it) and seen the way you went off on that sneaky snakey Thelma behind...what was it?"

My smoke-enclosed brain struggled to recall. "Oh yeah. She tried to take my toothpaste." I had told her, when I'd caught her slipping it from out of my foot locker, that if it was hers, the way she'd had the amazing gall to claim, then I'd like to see her stick it up her ass and squeeze it. And then go ahead and brush her teeth.

"Yeh. After that, I said to myself," Gloria cupped her cheek in her hand and rolled her eyes skyward, "I said Oooo-weee, this baby has got to be carrying, and knowing how to use whatever it is, because nobody that size would otherwise have the nerve."

I did have my knife, but I kept it under my blankets; and really, I was too afraid to use it—though naturally I wouldn't tell Gloria, or anybody else, as much.

"Well shit," I said. "I mean damn. Stealing my toothpaste, right in front of me. And telling me it's hers. She's the one with nerve. Who'd she think she was?"

Gloria rolled her head and shook with laughter. "I don't know. I guess somebody's God done told Thelma that she's slick." Gloria slapped her knee. "And then she hands that tube right back to you, when anyone else woulda had a scrape on their hands. Guess she figured the same thing about you that I did—this girl must got some big-time backup to be acting this way."

I giggled. I loved it when people told me how big and bold I was, and hated it just as much when people told me that I wasn't.

"I must have been high," I admitted once I'd stopped my giggling. Marijuana made me fearless, or mindless of the consequences, which amounted to the same effect.

Gloria sobered. "Yeah well, girlfriend, let me give you one hint: anyone who acts like you and isn't able to back it up isn't nothing but a sucker."

"I can back it up." I lifted my arm and pulled a muscle. I was rough, tough and strong. Anybody who thought I was sweet was going to have another think.

Gloria snorted. "That ain't hardly what I'm talking about, child. Where are you from?"

"From Baltimore. But why?"

"I'm trying to figure where you got this idea that you can say and do whatever to whoever and not get any trouble for it."

I had to think about that one. "Well." I poked a hole into the dust with my thumb, then gazed out over the fence that Gloria leaned against. "It's from my family."

Gloria's gaze was steady. "Yeh?" she asked quietly, expectantly. Her eyes were so much like Tammy's in this moment, demanding an explanation as though she had a friendly right to it. Was it true that girlfriends, like Gloria and Tammy were to me, really were entitled to the story of my sad and boring little life? Was this a black thing I didn't know about, dues that needed to be left beside the gate of rite of passage? An explanation was the answer, demanded, to the usually-silent question that I saw inside the eyes of every black person I ever spent any kind of time with—How you got to be this way, white girl? So tough, so foolish, so much like us, so much unlike us.

What the hell, I was high enough; I could forget any words, even words of truth, as soon as they came out of my mouth. I took a huge, long breath. "I had to learn to defend myself somehow. It seemed like they could say and do anything to me, and then use some apology as an excuse: 'Oh, I'm sorry, I only said that because I was so upset at the time.' But at the time you said it, you said you meant it, so what am I supposed to believe? Or, 'Oh, I'm sorry, please forgive me, I was drunk at the time.' Fuck!" One time, after twelve martinis—I had counted his trips to the liquor cabinet—my father had suggested that, since I didn't have a boyfriend, I ought to learn to fuck myself. "You wanna watch or something?" I'd replied, casually, though my shamed gaze had shied away from him. Infuriated, he slapped me.

I viciously ripped a dandelion out of the ground. These fucking dandelions, along with crabgrass, were the only things that grew around here. I threw the dandelion head against the fence. "Those people drove me crazy."

Gloria looked confused. "Why you say it just like that: 'those people'? Was you adopted?"

I glowered. "Yeah," I lied, "By the sorriest people in the world." "Sorry" was a word that Tammy used to describe certain people; and when she used it, I knew exactly what she was talking about. "Sorry" was my father, asking my mother's forgiveness for the drinking that he knew he wasn't going to stop—and for all the things he wasn't going to stop when he was drunk, and conveniently couldn't remember when he was sober. "Sorry" was my mother the nurse cleaning up the blood and vomit and shattered glass and flesh until the next round—and then forgiving him, until the next round.

"In my house," I bit the words off, "When a person said they were sorry, they meant it."

Gloria's laughter was warm and soothing. "Shit, girl, you have not seen sorry until you seen some of my people. Last time I talked to Moms, she tried to borrow money from me. Me, with this little bit of chump change that I makes round here. When I was a child, Daddy brought his girlfriend in to stay with us, and Moms was sorry enough never to have minded, because Daddy would have hit the spit out of her had she much as breathed one mumbling word. That shit's still going on, only now it's my sisters doing her wrong. Last I heard, they stole her check last Mother's Day, but you know Moms—she'll go swear, all up and down, that they aren't on the needle."

I sighed; that was the problem with this prison: whatever horror story you had, everybody else had at least one that was worse. "Well, how about this," I asked, "My father gave all my family's savings to some prostitute. And then was sorry enough to ask me for understanding because this woman was 'more fun' than my mother was." My stomach clenched; it was something I had never admitted to anyone, least of all to Tammy. It must have been the weed that was talking. Maybe by tomorrow, if this weed was strong enough, we'd both forget I'd ever said it.

Yet Gloria was laughing again. "Mm mm." Her eyes were gleaming. "That's some action I sure would of liked to get over onto, back in my days."

"This one was white," I snapped. (Oh my God! I couldn't believe I'd said something so prejudiced.)

Gloria lifted her dimpled, ample chin up toward the sky and laughed even harder. "Yep. I bet your daddy wouldn't touch no nigger who' wid no ten-foot pole. Rather have him one of those ugly, skinny hipless ones who do it like they need the practice."

I guffawed. Loudly. To hide my shame, and also because it really was hilarious as hilarity can be, only when you're high. My father, sorry as he was, thought that he was better than everybody, anybody black. Hilarious and ironic that here I sat, ashamed because of this small piece, all mine, of behavior I had thought was his. Hilarious and ironic that here I sat, in prison.

How you ended up here? It was the question I saw in every other inmate's eyes the whole first month I was in. Except that Gloria had come right out and asked it: "So how did you ever end up in here?"

I had stammered my reply: "It was a mix-up. I was set up. It was a mistake." The biggest mistake of my life.

Gloria had snorted. "Child, that's what we all say."

Unfortunately, my joint has gone out. Frantically, I hunt up another book of matches; and feel a relief that suffuses me like a giant hit when I find one underneath my notebook. I re-light, and draw as deeply as I can, and stretch back onto my bed. Chill out, I instruct myself, as the hot smoke hits and cools my brain. Just chill; it's over now, I reach for my radio, and turn it on.

> *Always and forever,*
> *each moment with you*

Aaah. Euphoria, all over again.

I take another toke.

"Beth, I don't mean to be critical or nothing," Tammy had begun one night, one mid-semester, when I had smoked myself somnambulant, "but don't you think you been smokin an awful lot lately?"

"No. I don't."

She'd looked hurt, but doggedly continued. "Now, I can

tell that something's bothering you, though Lord in Heaven knows you never let on what —

"My parents are finally getting a divorce."

Tammy's face had softened into sadness. More sadness, in fact, than the occasion warranted.

"And I'm glad," I said.

"Then why you smokin so much?" she quietly asked. I'd shrugged.

"Think of what you're doing to your mind."

"I'm giving my mind some ease." Otherwise it would have run me ragged and bloody. Especially at night, when I wanted to sleep.

"But sister, you are so smart. And talented."

"Would you lay off?"

Tammy's cheeks tightened; she looked away. "Sorry. I won't say nothing more."

Oh God. I'd hurt her, something I'd never done before. All of my smoke-induced oblivion dissolved, like fog beneath unwelcome sun. Tammy wasn't used to being yelled and sworn at. Compared to me, Tammy had been protected. I'd said the very same thing my father said, to hurt my mother, every time she tried to coax him out of one more shot, glass, can, swallow, one more trip to the liquor store. But I was not going to be like him. It was one vow I'd made myself before I'd left his house.

I reached for Tammy's hand. "I'm sorry. I'll stop smoking so much." But that was exactly like my father, too; couldn't I do any better? "You're just like your father," was the one accusation I would never forgive my mother for. No less because I'd refused to understand it. I hadn't "lost" one dollar of her money.

I drew a breath and groped for Tammy's other hand. And couldn't find another thing to say: because how would I ever keep the promise I'd just made?

On the radio, "Always and Forever" is ending; it is a song so romantic, it always makes me sad.

I roll over and snuff my joint out. The shit isn't working anyhow; I'm not feeling the way I'm supposed to, or at least not the way I want to. Because I'm feeling miserable, and I know it. What will happen when I tell Tammy how I ended up in prison? What will I say, where will my battered feelings run to, if she tells me I deserved every minute of my one to six-month indeterminate sentence? How will I forgive her if she shows one sign of being like every other person who tried to lay some claim to loving me?

Rude Awakening

by Lynn Alldrin

Have you ever walked around in somebody else's feet?
It happens after a night of too much of the bottle
and too much of the man, wearing clothes that grab
your crotch too tight and hair bleached too blonde,
and eyelashes heavy as tarred black feathers.
Then a woman wonders whose feet are down there, carrying
her fatally into the smoky mirrors, tritely marching her
    through
a soap opera that looks like somebody else's life sliced
open for the birds to pick clean.

surrendering to the crash

by Pamela Gray

i

"Don't you think people notice the wine bottles on top of your refrigerator?"

"What are you talking about?"

"It's a cry for help. It's obvious."

"I haven't had a chance to recycle them; that's all."

"It's a cry for help."

"I don't know what you're talking about."

ii

there are no boundaries i can do anything to her body she can do anything to my body somehow we are in a bubble bath and there is only candlelight and everywhere is heat and wetness and the taste of gin and somehow now we are in her room and somehow i can't tell which is her body and which is mine and i am opening opening opening and nothing matters i would do anything and it wouldn't matter.

iii

donna summer is always in the background. i sit at the bar and wait for something to happen. what am i waiting for? something. i drink another gin and tonic. i am part of this crowd; i am not part of this crowd. i want someone to approach me; i pray no one approaches me. there is no place i'd rather be i want to go home. i drink another gin and tonic. i stand at the edge of the dance floor. the women take their shirts off and dance in a circle. their breasts are beautiful in the dim light of the back room. they are moving as one, connected to each other, donna summer's voice traveling through their bodies, or, rather, through their one circular body. i am trapped at the edge and can't move into the circle. there are miles and miles between me and the circle, i want to be in the circle, i no longer know how i wound up on this edge. i drink another gin and tonic.

iv

where is the entrance? how do i get on the 93? wait—is this...? wait—is this...? no, that way is charlestown but which way is somerville? wait—oh god where's the road where's the ramp where is it where is it how do i get home? how do i get home?

v

red wine and more red wine and more red wine and more and my body can hardly move my body slides into hers my body is so lazy my body is liquid

you make me sick i'm gonna leave your ass i must be crazy to be with you

what? what's going on here? wait! why are you talking to me like that?

i could kill you right now i feel like strangling you like sticking a knife in your chest

i don't...i don't understand. why are you yelling at me? what happened? a minute ago we were...

take me home i have to get away from you

but i can't i can't drive i had too much to drink what's going on? why are you...?

you fucking bitch take me home

don't leave me don't leave me don't

vi

she orders another bottle. she pours herself another glass. she pours me another glass. light glistens in the white wine, in her hair; the thin slices of yellow apple sit untouched on the plate. she talks and talks. too much. i am trying to listen but all i can focus on is the light. another glass. another glass. fibers of gold light spin around us and we are cocooned, enfolded, wine and talk spin around me and nothing matters anymore, this night can swallow me up and i wouldn't care. the fibers snap: she pulls me out of the restaurant and into her sports car, and she is driving too fast, too fast, and she is still talking, too fast, too fast, and the lights on the freeway pull me toward them and i can hardly breathe enough to say slow down and i surrender myself to the crash i imagine comes next.

vii

a parking lot. her fingers in my hair. tugging. her teeth in my shoulder. my nails in her back. she grabs my breast. i grab between her legs. is this passion? is this rage? my heart races. we are in that cocoon again but the fibers are not light; the fibers are barbed wire and we claw at each other to get out. fear is the heart pulsing inside this cocoon and alcohol is the blood that feeds the heart, that feeds the fear, that feeds us, that feeds us. we tear free of each other and stumble into the bar for more.

viii

in the morning the sun filters through the gold and yellow open-weave curtains, casting hexagons of light onto the maple kitchen table. the green wine bottles glisten on top of the refrigerator. i stare at them as the coffee brews. one. two. three. four. five. six. seven. eight. nine. ten. eleven. how long did it take me? i don't remember. why does it give me a sense of accomplishment? what have i accomplished?

ix

"Do you realize how many times you mentioned getting drunk this week?"

"What?"

"You seem to get drunk several times a week."

"No. Just this week, maybe."

"It seems like every time you come in here, you mention going out drinking and getting drunk."

"Look. That's not what I came here to talk about."

The Art of Blacking Out

by Annie Dawid

A tooth in a tube
like a seed in ether
sprouts on the windowsill.
There are reasons for the absence of mirrors.
A miracle: I was someone else before.
Now I am naked, new beneath the gown,
a white room over a blue lake
where canoes glide smoothly
to catch the season's last sun
on mute green bows.

To lose twelve hours
is to lose your life.
Found: one bruised boozer
and a hangover of spectral hues,
grenadine, green, the piss yellow
of weak beer colors flesh beneath my eye.
They ask if I know my name, age,
day of the week, how many fingers.
How much does it matter?
I tell them everything,
which is not enough.

Because I cannot remember, I invent:
some other woman leading some other life,
rich with hope.
The nurses are not fooled.
They warn me I am not pretty,
but imagine I am brave.

Looking down at the body battered
is one thing, suture hanging
like darning thread,
but to see yourself reflected
is head-on collision

I have not been beaten,
hit by a car, or damaged
by any other thing.
The other woman smiles,
offers her great, gaping hole.

absinthe

by Melissa Cannon

                absinthe
dark stars
                        glitter
        showers
                    of jet
            blood
                        exploding
            roses
        nights
            i suck
                    anger
oblivion
        from my obsidian
        bottle
        swirl
                in the black
            glass
mornings
                    after
        have teeth
                    of bitter
            chalk
heaving
            too-bright light
        like jackhammer
and i wake
                    and know
                i
        am my own
            poison

The Oath

by Joan Connor

Shrouds draped the furniture in the living room. The room smelled of mothballs. Only 4:30, but the house was already dusky. In October in the mountains, the sun could be stingy. Paula flicked the wall switch without much hope. The wall sconces leapt with light. The power hadn't been disconnected yet. She snuggled Jesse under her arm and crossed the room, pulled the drawer out of the bottom of the blanket chest, wrapped her son in a blanket and nestled him into the drawer.

The summer house was cold, the furnace shut down, the pipes drained, the phone disconnected. Her parents were abroad. If Perry tried to call her, he wouldn't be able to get through. She'd return home in a day or two. She always returned. But first she would worry Perry, make him think that this time she would not be back. Perhaps he would take her seriously then. Perhaps then Perry would stop the endless haggling over money. She wondered if he would be home from work yet, if he had found her note. She hadn't wanted to worry him too much. "I need to get away," she'd written. "I've taken Jesse. I'll call after I've had some time to think." She hadn't signed it. Who else would it be from?

She checked on the baby. Jesse was still sleeping, his small fist balled in his mouth. One place was the same as another to him, a place to sleep. But she wondered if he were warm enough. She'd read about SIDS, the possibility sudden death might be caused by cold drafts or lying on the stomach. She slipped her hands under his shoulders, settling his back, and checked his breathing.

Crossing to the hearth, she opened the damper to a whoosh of cold, ashy air, crumpled some paper and cabined the kindling. She struck a match. The fire caught. When she tossed on a log, the birch paper peeled off in flaming curls, snapping. It was cold. She could feel the chill pressing its firm, dark hands on her jacketed shoulders. But alcohol didn't freeze. She rose and opened the door to the liquor cabinet, poured Cointreau, dark rum, some whiskey and gin into a tumbler. Taste didn't matter. She drank for effect.

The next morning she came to on the wicker couch, swaddled in a shroud. She squinted. Morning sun, sharp as glass shatters, sprayed from the long windows. Jesse was babbling beside her on the floor. Paula wanted to kiss him, but she didn't dare lower her head which felt as thin and brittle as an eggshell. Suddenly and fully awake, but confused in that temporary displacement peculiar to tourists and drunks, she asked herself—where am I? How did I get here? She reconstructed the drive to Vermont, mixing the zombie cocktails, leaving the note. Yes, but the incidents came back to her out of sequence, runny. Somewhere inside her raddled consciousness this thought floated, intact as a yolk: you should not be subjecting Jesse to this. But she did not clarify the object of the pronoun—this what? Just a vague, queasy guilt. Gingerly, she turned her head toward Jesse and smiled. Her tongue unglued from the roof of her mouth, "Morning, baby Jess." He chuckled and grabbed for her finger.

Reaching, she knocked over the empty tumbler beside her on the floor. How much had she had to drink? She propped her head up. She couldn't keep doing this. Jess was getting older. She swung her legs off the couch and stared at the cold, sooty fireplace. An ember had burned out dangerously close to the wood floor, leaving a small char mark like a cigarette burn. She stretched. Her skin felt as rumpled and dirty as the clothes she'd slept in.

Stocking-footed, she padded to the kitchen, noted the open tuna cans and an opener among the bottles. At least she'd had the good sense to eat something. But through the impenetrability of the blackout, she really could not be sure. A midnight stranger could have slipped in, fixed a meal and slipped out. Then she realized that she was that stranger. She wondered if, sober, she'd recognize herself, a body on automatic pilot attending to its needs and functions. She had a cut on her index finger. She couldn't remember how it had happened. The thought that she could trespass in her own family house, that she could, alien, possess herself unnerved her. Demon rummy.

Remorseful, bruised, she screwed the caps back on the bottles, promising herself she would not drink again. She stashed the bottles back in the liquor cabinet and rinsed the tuna cans in some water from the bucket. Water. She must have made a midnight run to the springhouse as well. She poured some of it into a saucepan and heated formula on the stove for Jess.

Only after she'd fed Jess his bottle and changed him and was searching for Tylenol in the medicine cabinet, did she notice the bent prong on her ring. The setting gaped. The stone was gone. She stared at the prong, twisted up but slightly askew like a crooked spire.

Her hangover vanished. She slammed the medicine cabinet shut and stared at herself in the mirror. She'd lost her ruby. What would Perry say? He'd be furious. Just one more unnecessary expense. Just one more example of her irresponsibility. How many times had he told her to keep the ring in the jewelry box except for special occasions? Perry, who always counted his change before leaving any store. Perry, who never paid before he was served even at MacDonald's. Perry who calculated the best buy on paper towels by the ply and the number of squares per roll. She'd have to find the stone.

She pawed through the couch cushions, found two pennies and a quarter—not enough to buy a mood ring, let alone a ruby. She checked the recycling bin where she'd tossed the tuna cans. Crawling on the floor, she groped through dust kitties. She raked through the fireplace ashes and emptied Jess's diaper bag. She tried to remember which rooms she'd been in the night before, but her third drink had dropped a shroud on her memory which she couldn't raise. Jesse fussed. Her irritability and panic rose with his wails, Why was a baby's scream so insistent—a biological telephone call, so impersonal, so impossible to ignore ringing, ringing in the cradle, a computerized telemarketing call? No disconnect. Maybe he was still hungry. She mashed a banana in a bowl, fed him, and settled him back in the drawer.

Sitting next to him on the floor, she searched her memory. Small facets of the previous night flashed at her, tiny glints: water sloshing her thigh as she dragged the pail up the hill, the fire flaring as she burned an angry letter she'd written to Perry on her mother's stationery, the car door slamming into her shoulder as she'd retrieved her overnight bag. She went outside to search the car, but the search yielded nothing but candy wrappers and a gummy pacifier. Back inside the house, she jostled the bottles in the liquor cabinet again, groped the baseboards in the kitchen, re-checked the couch cushions.

As she searched, the ruby grew smaller and smaller. How could she ever find such a tiny stone? It could be anywhere inside her parents' house or outside in the frostbitten grass or under a crumpled leaf. No matter what Perry said the stone was worth, it wasn't worth this desperation. It was hopeless. Her knees and elbows smudged with dust, she looked at Jesse. "It's no good, Jess," she said. "I'm never going to find it." But Jesse was asleep.

What was she doing here with her baby in a cold and enormous summer house in October, conducting a futile search for a tiny stone? She no longer felt angry with Perry. Fear nudged her anger aside, then hopelessness, then shame, then contrition.

She poured herself a drink and sat on the couch to relax, but she couldn't keep her eyes from straying to the floor, scouting the oriental rug for the ruby. So much red in its maze-like geometric pattern. So much red. Her hands fidgeted with the cushions. I know it's here, she told herself, I know that stone's somewhere in this house. She paced and poked, and searched. And the more she searched, the more frantic she became, and the more frantic she became, the more she searched—and the more she drank.

Maudlin drunk, lonely and cold, she lifted her glass and declared, "I've got to find that stone. God, please help me find it, and I swear I'll..." She squinted at her glass. "I'll stop drinking. I swear it. Please let me find the stone." Pledging aloud relieved her. She smiled; she was going to stop drinking. She drained her glass.

Paula woke up in the morning thinking, enough of this. She splashed water on the ashes in the fireplace, shut the damper. She was going to go home. She changed Jess, then went to the kitchen to heat water to mix some wheat cereal. As she twisted the knob on the stove, a red sparkle flashed in the corner of her eye.

No, she thought, no, then, yes. But it couldn't be. She pressed her fingertip down on the sparkle feeling its hardness. She fingered it, lifted it. Yes, it was her ruby. How had she missed it yesterday? Gratitude and elation flowed into the hollows worn by yesterday's hysteria. The sun spilled over the windowsill. "My ruby, Jess, my ruby," she yelled. The baby chuckled. It was like a miracle. She tore off a corner of paper towel, carefully wrapped the ruby and tucked it into her change purse.

Perry accepted her when she arrived home. They talked. He apologized for losing his temper. Resetting the ruby cost $75, an amount he deducted from her household budget. She didn't object; it was a small price to pay. Nor did she tell Perry about her oath. He wasn't a religious man. But, true to her word, she didn't drink. Not for two weeks.

In the second week after they'd reconciled, she and Perry fought over money again. He wanted to sell one of the cars. The insurance was too expensive. "But I need a car," she argued. "What if something happened to Jess? What if there were an emergency?"

"Dial 911," Perry said and he placed a classified ad over the phone.

The night Perry sold the car, she poured herself a glass of wine. Just one glass, she told herself. I won't break my oath, exactly. I won't get drunk. Just one glass.

Later, she hid the empty wine bottle in the bottom of the recycling bin under the empty jars of mayonnaise and peanut butter, where she'd always hid her bottles in the past. If Perry found them, she could tell him she'd picked them up on the roadside when she'd taken Jess for a stroll. Litter. She went to bed early.

Every time she drank, on all the mornings after, she swore she would not drink again. For Jess, she told herself, for Jess whose birth had surprised her with joy, whose ten fingers and ten toes she counted small miracles. And every time she did drink, she swore it would be just one glass.

She would try not to drink, then break her promise. Sodden with guilt and remorse, she'd manage a week of sobriety, two. For Jess, she said, for Perry. Then furious with Perry, she'd sling Jess into his Snugli, hike to the grocery store, buy a magnum of cheap red wine, drink it all and go to bed early after settling Jess for the night, fuming at Perry—how could he not know? How could he not know?

At three in the morning she'd wake with a start, Perry snoring beside her, as she stared open-eyed at the dark ceiling with insomniac dread. She'd sworn to God she would not drink. She'd sworn to the ultimate eavesdropper who could read minds, the ultimate peeping Tom who saw her when she could not even see herself. And she'd broken her oath. "Forgive me," she prayed in the dark. "Forgive me. I'll try harder." Only to break the oath again and again.

Perry no longer told her to keep the ring in the jewelry box. She could not bear to wear it. Its ruby drew a thorn's pinprick of blood.

Sometimes, alone, when she warmed the bowl of the wine goblet in her palms, she thought that perhaps finding the ruby was no miracle after all. Just coincidence. The ruby had simply dropped from the setting as she'd opened a can of tuna, and, in her panicky search, she'd overlooked it. It was such a small ruby and obviously a faulty setting. A cheap ring, really. The whole thing was Perry's fault if you thought about it—buying her such a shoddy engagement ring. No miracle at all. Just two accidents. Random. The ruby lost, the ruby found. She sipped the gem-like lucidity, the burgundy glow of her wine.

But on other nights she woke from red-tinged nightmares. Red as fire, red as sin. I've sinned, she told herself over and over, against God, against myself. But no, she calmed herself. He is mercy, the wine-blood of forgiveness. He would forgive her. It was okay to drink if she didn't get drunk, okay to drink if she only drank twice a month, maybe, or once a week. Unable to fall back asleep, she'd wander downstairs for a nightcap.

She turned the oath over and over in her mind so light would catch its every possibility: that the recovery of the stone was a coincidence, that God would forgive her, that she could forgive herself, that she still might reform, that there was no god, that the initial loss of the stone was Perry's fault. But she no longer raged privately at Perry—how could he not know—because he did know. He pleaded, he threatened, he smashed her bottles on the deck floor, staining the planks with red-brown blots the rains could not wash away. And when he threatened to take Jess from her, she prayed, "Please God, don't take Jess away from me. Don't take Jess, and I will..." But what was there to say? What contingency to promise, to break?

And, only later, after she'd lost Jesse and Perry, after she'd gone to Lazarus House for the third time to dry out, did she consider the final possibility—she'd condemned herself. She had lifted her glass. She had initiated the terms of the covenant she could not keep.

The red, sharp nightmares no longer cut into her sleep. She sacrificed her conscience. She sacrificed the god she knew could not forgive her since she alone had sworn and betrayed her oath. She sacrificed everything that had ever mattered to her except the small, red hardness that centered her.

When she met her counselor for her daily session, she quietly explained, "I want to check out. I'm a voluntary here."

The woman murmured her objection, consulted a file, riffled some pages. "Lazarus came back from the dead; you can, too. That's the point of Lazarus House, a second chance."

Paula only smiled. She'd been hearing the Lazarus tale cited as a resurrection myth for years, but she knew it was a horror story, that Lazarus had awakened, his mouth full of dirt, earthy with the knowledge of death, and he'd stepped back out into the world, choking on soil, spitting, knowing that dark place, knowing that he would again go back there, his eyes wide open.

"But why do you want to leave?" her counselor demanded.

Paula sat still. She was the still center of the room. Pronged and empty.

"Certainly you don't think you're cured."

She shook her head. She could see it in the corner of her eye, glinting with remarkable clarity. The truth, blood-red as her own blood, glittering inside in the setting from which it could never be prized free. It had always been there. It would always be. Original.

"No, I don't think I'm cured," she said. And she added simply, "I'm damned."

A Favor

by Michelle M. Tokarczyk

There were too many years
when I'd walk from bars
unsteadily to street lamps
on a block I'd recognize
as mine.

But this one night:

I reached for my key,
found him at my side.
I didn't know why.
He came in, even held me
as I cried.

I went to lie down. He
stretched beside me
on too narrow a couch.
I threw up. He cleaned up,
returned, unbuttoned my
blouse,
unzipped my pants. I said no—
I'd get pregnant.
He put my hand on his cock.
I said I was too tired.
He said it wouldn't take long.
(I guess it didn't.)

When he left he copied
my number off the phone.
When he called he reminded me
he'd cleaned up.

Recovery:
Out of the Maze

Answer to a Dionysian Adventurer

by Zoe Keithley

Go
Into the dark.
See, we open the door.

Go
Into the cleft
Into the pitch
Into the deafening silence
And the terrible roar.

Go
But first feel
There
And there,
Around you,
The lassos of our love
To bring you back.

Fragments Becoming Whole

by Julie Novak-McSweeney

Waking Dream:

> *I am thirteen, in my nightgown, walking to the bath-room. I close the door behind me. Before I can turn on the light, my father grabs me—he has been hiding in the dark behind the door. He pushes my nightgown up around my neck. I start to struggle and he hurts me. "None of that," he hisses. "Be quiet. Be quiet."*

I break the surface of this nightmare, a swimmer gasping for air. This dream is not fantasy, but memory. Recollections of childhood are deep waters for me. Until recently I only dared enter them during sleep, lest they become a drowning pool.

For eleven years, until one day in my fifteenth year, my father sexually and emotionally abused me. He was an alcoholic and a capricious, violent disciplinarian. Perhaps my mother and grandmother were afraid to openly challenge him, or were ignorant of what was really happening. Whatever their motives, they did little to protect me.

Like many other abused children, I survived by adopting a protective amnesia. There are years of childhood forever lost to me, or existing only as random puzzle pieces. I feel as though I'm searching a house's blasted wreckage after a fire; I sift the cooling ashes to find one precious thing intact. Or as though I'm pursuing the trailing edge of a robe as it disappears around a corner. I want to meet the robed one, but the more I pursue, the more she eludes me. I have learned to sit patiently and let the memories come to me, like cats or shy children.

For years I kept a safe and total distance from my child-hood. My intent was self-protection, but my denial of the truth kept me trapped and wandering in an emotional cul-de-sac. True self-protection for me now lies in my struggle to understand and break free of the old patterns, the fear and victimization.

Charting my way through the blind alley of amnesia and silence is the work of a lifetime.

I am learning to remember, and to speak.

How to begin to find a voice? I have spent an exhausted week in bed with laryngitis, indulging in my first love: reading. Even so, I've been depressed and frustrated. I realized today how this illness mirrors my childhood: the chronic fatigue, the inability to speak, the powerlessness. As a child, I read constantly. Books were a wonderful escape into a world in which mothers were affectionate to their daughters, where fathers were loving, sometimes stern, but never alcoholic or violent. All this "normality" seemed truly exotic compared to the realities of life in our household.

Silence. I tried to say as little as possible in my father's presence. To attract his notice was usually to provoke his wrath—or, worse, his sexual attentions. At dinner, his presence was an avalanche that threatened to bury us all. Night after night my brother alone would show signs of life, doing or saying something that made dad angry enough to beat him. I took my cues from my mother and grandmother. They rarely attempted to intervene in my father's dealings with "his" children; they would eat silently or talk to each other instead. My father would often shoulder his way into their talk and quash it somehow. Then we would sit and eat, mute as the flowers on our plastic tablecloth. I learned young that to let the avalanche bury me in silence was to be invisible, was to survive.

So many terrifying experiences to "forget" back then. Father's hands grabbing me as I ran playing in the yard. Fingers stuck in my panties, or a spanking for some minute infraction of his ever-changing rules. Hands invading my body's privacy at all hours of the day and night. Unasked-for "help" during my nightly bath. "Someone" creeping through my darkened bedroom as I held my breath and pretended to be asleep. The family fiction was that I was overimaginative, impressionable, prone to nightmares.

There are many ways to lie.

I grew up thinking all families must be like mine, a cluster of countries engaged in constant border wars.

Guerrilla action was possible. The midnight visits stopped when I was fifteen. I had by this time developed a pathological fear of "burglars" breaking into our house after dark. At bedtime one night I was inspired to push my desk up against my door, preventing outside access to my bedroom. My family did not comment.

I waited to be seventeen. The hope of going away to college sustained me.

I had mixed feelings about leaving home. Although I breathed more freely outside my father's house, I was awkward in this new social world composed solely of my peers. My most primal relationship—the one with my father—was based on his absolute power over me. I duplicated this pattern in my relationships at school—it wasn't enjoyable, but it certainly was familiar. I sought out people who would dominate me. They were always forceful, charismatic personalities who were alternately abusive and withdrawn. If I met someone who showed me real tenderness or affection, I despised them for their vulnerability, just as I hated myself for my childhood helplessness against my father's will.

When I slept alone, I would awaken several times during the night. Heart pounding, I would stare into the persistent darkness, nearly suffocated by a fear for which I had no name. There seemed to be no safety in solitude, so I began spending all my time with others. I became sexually active with men, involving myself in a series of relatively brief relationships. I didn't enjoy sex much. I would "split off", my consciousness hovering over the bed while my body cooperated with my partner's desire. This is supposed to be fun, I would remind myself miserably. Why can't I enjoy this? Nevertheless, the distress (and often boredom) of sex was a small price to pay for the nighttime comfort of another's presence.

One night, some friends took me out drinking. I had never been to a bar before. That night I saw people drinking to have fun, to loosen up and forget themselves. Forget themselves. I drank all the scotches I could hold. I had never felt so relaxed, talkative and happy. The next day, my boyfriend told me I had been a "wild woman" in bed that night. I couldn't remember anything I had said or done—but I remembered how good I had felt.

During the next ten years I graduated, entered my chosen profession, led an active social life and drank myself into a stupor every chance I got. When I was drunk, it didn't matter that I was painfully shy—with a drink in my hand I could talk to anyone (and often did). It wasn't important that I feared and hated sex—four or five drinks taught me to love it. So what if I couldn't remember much of my childhood? If pressed for details, I would invent them, basing my fictions on books I'd read in childhood. I resurrected my grandmother's long-dead alcoholic husband and recast him as the kindly grandfather from Heidi. Mom became the wise and loving Marmee from Little Women, while I reshaped my father into a sort of working-class Atticus Finch, the lawyer-father from To Kill a Mockingbird. I rationalized my "poor memory" and told myself that whatever I made up was probably more entertaining to me and my listener than whatever had actually happened.

There are many ways to lie. My family taught me well. I lied about everything—my past, my present feelings—and I kept drinking.

I was so desperately lonely that I remember slipping away from a tableful of friends in a bar to go into the bathroom and cry. Moments like these bewildered me. I must be crazy to feel so lonely, confused and sad. Didn't I have a great job? friends? lovers?

I drifted or trudged through a series of relationships with emotionally abusive/neglectful men. I was always careful to choose partners who were not prone to physical violence. I also made sure they drank as much as, or more than, I did. We called it "serious recreational drinking". The sex afterwards was passionate, wild. It was the only time I felt confident of my partner's attention and regard, and my own worth. There would be fights marked by insults and mockery. I never admitted how hurt I was by these fights. I was afraid that my emotions would shatter me like glass, that I would bleed to death on my own loneliness and need.

As a victim, I knew by heart the pattern of abuse, pain, isolation. I wandered for years in a familiar, invisible fog.

The barrier to my sexual and emotional fulfillment, I decided, was the Midwest. Desiring to live where I could have joyous, stimulating, perfect relationships, I moved to California. What I found, however, was that the snares of habit and history did not let go so easily. Even when I met loving partners, the intimacy they offered was too foreign; it confused me, even as I yearned for it. They tried, I tried, we'd break up, come together, break up—drinking every step of the way.

I had the vague sense that something was wrong with my life. I was seldom sober and began having frequent blackouts. I had used alcohol to block out the memories of incest so that I could sexually function as an adult. Now alcohol had turned on me—there were things I wanted to remember, and couldn't. I struggled to control my intake, and drank more than ever. My eventual decision to quit drinking, a day at a time, grew out of my willingness to swim the deep and silent waters of childhood memory.

When I got sober, two things happened: I became celibate, and my sleeping patterns changed dramatically. As a drinker, I used to put myself to sleep with cognac every night. Now I reverted to anxious insomnia, waking at three a.m., often needing a light on before I could fall asleep again. Then the nightmares began, terrifying dreams about my father coming into my bedroom, grabbing me as I ran down dark hallways, violating me. I could never scream, could barely struggle against him, and would wake up sobbing and confused. I came to understand that these nightmares were memories from childhood. Frightening as these dreams can be, they are precious bits of my childhood, lost fragments trying to become whole.

I began to have true friendships, to learn a whole new set of relationship skills. Honesty. Openness. Willingness, to listen and to talk, to trust. Being afraid, and going ahead.

A chance meeting one day with an acquaintance became dinner, blossomed into a love affair and, a year later, marriage. Never have I felt such joy, such safety with another person. Never in my life have I struggled so hard to reclaim my body's right to give and receive pleasure.

A survivor is willing to remember, and to speak.

Many, many times my body yields up memories, bitter and painful. One by one, my love and I exorcise my father-demons and fill new space with light, passion, joy.

My body is sacred. My breasts, my womb are sacred.

I am an adult woman, living in her body, and in present time.

Waking Dream:

I am on a bicycle. I wheel across the mountain at wild sunset, sped by wind and color. As night claims the sky, I come to a familiar house. The door is open and I enter. Something, someone lurking...my throat constricts...No! I scream with all my strength.

To my surprise, there is now a rattle in my hand. I shake it as I move through the house. In a bedroom is my father, asleep. I move to his side and do what I must. In a violent and ritual act of power, I bring the rattle down with force upon his skull. His bones splinter into dust.

Night Bridges

by Jean Walton Wolf

The one thing I don't want to do, going to Big Sur, is to drive there after dark. I've seen pictures of the sheer and sharp cliffs, resplendent in mist and crashing waves, and I am afraid to drive the narrow, winding coast highway for the first time alone in the dark. I am pushing myself, then, when I leave Oakland at four.

Fremont and San Jose traffic Friday afternoon is hot and crowded. My neck and back are stiff and damp, and I have to turn the radio up loud to fight off drowsiness. I am drugged and hypnotised by the monotony of driving. I shake myself alert to keep from drifting into the dusty aluminum side of a truck in the lane next to me.

By the time I reach Monterey and Highway 1, the sun is setting behind the bay and my headlights are on. It is quiet in the car going through Carmel, and it is getting darker quickly. The light is green at Rio Road. Once out of town I floor it. I am glad the road ahead is empty. For some reason I remember Pa's story from *Little House on the Prairie* about galloping home the night the panther chased him in the dark, leaping overhead him from tree to tree. I urge the car on, swooping over the first rolling curves on the coast road. The sky is deepening blue-black like a bruise, and there is one last faint breath of orange fading on the horizon. Any other time it would be a beautiful sight, but tonight I barely take a hurried peek at this richness. I have somewhere to be, and to me this road is no friend.

The gentle curving hills give way to the first sheer cliffs as the sky becomes night. I check my map. Forty-five miles to go.

I set the trip odometer, and feel my spirits sink. I remember the first time I went to Big Sur. I was five and with my family. We had lunch at Nepenthe, the restaurant on the cliffs. Nepenthe, the elixir of alcohol and drugs, killer of pain. I remember sitting with my family at a table in the sun close to the edge of the cliff. There were sparkly hanging decorations overhead. Later the square black and white photo pasted in the album showed a 1950s family of four. My father still looked young and tall, my brother and I dangled our legs in the air, and my mother was calm but distant. She had been a Maui girl, born and raised near the red dirt of a Hawaiian sugar plantation, the first one from her town of Puunene to go to Vassar. She still talks about the time her father forbade her to go to law school, so she moved to San Francisco and met my father. She lives alone in Honolulu now and wears glasses to hide the bags under her yellow eyes, unfocussed from the bourbon always on hand.

I see the bridge ahead. It is graceful and eerie, even in the dark. I cannot believe how high it is. My palms tingle and go damp as I clutch the steering wheel tighter. When my tires cross onto the bridge my fear becomes near panic. I think of horses who refuse to step onto flimsy surfaces, or babies who won't cross Plexiglass suspended in the air. For an instant I am afraid I will lose control. I am terrified my hands will spin to the right without my being able to stop them and that I won't be able to stay on this bridge. I pray. I concentrate. I force myself to focus on the road. I remind myself that I am a good driver, and that I trust my car. What I have feared has happened. I am driving the road to Big Sur alone and it is night.

The switchbacks and curves increase. I see sharp drops now. There are more bridges. I try not to think of earthquakes. I put in a tape. I don't care what it is. The recording is bad. I can barely hear it, but I am comforted by the sound.

Cars pass in the other direction. Some have their high beams on, but I am too afraid to move my hand from the steering wheel to flash my lights at them.

I pass the Ventana campground, where we stayed during the Nepenthe trip. I remember camping 30 years ago in the shade and dust, in an olive tent I never saw again. We left California shortly after that and we never returned, at least not together as a family. We spent the next thirteen years following my father's work, and we had adventures. We saw the east coast with gentle maple trees and thick snow at Christmas, then Panama with its hot and colorful streets. Then the years in Jamaica, with scrawny horses loping down dusty roads, and finally, Guatemala, where the mountain air was sweet and life was hard and sad. By that time we had moved away from each other and from ourselves. There were alcohol, fights and frightening nights alone in bed. My brother left home first, moving to Santa Barbara, then briefly to drugs and, later, to the desert, saying he didn't want to see the rest of us anymore. Within a few years there was nothing left. My parents divorced, and my father, who could never learn Spanish and who missed the sun, moved to Africa by himself. My mother was hospitalized for her drinking, the first of many times. And I was alone in Santa Cruz, trying to find myself in used, faded jeans and organic cashews from the Staff of Life. I never knew what to say to people when they asked me where I was from, or worse, where my family was now.

So tonight I am following this narrow black road. I have been afraid I will lose my way. I am afraid it will never end. I wonder why I have come here alone, and I cannot believe only twelve miles have passed. I grip the steering wheel and try not to think of spinning out over a rocky cliff, or where they would find my car.

I take a quick look at the night out my black window, and I am startled at how thick and rich the stars are now. There are no city lights around me. I cautiously slow down and pull the car over to a narrow, gravelled shoulder. I stop and get out. The wind is cold off the dark Pacific, the sea of peace, and the only sound is the waves crashing far below. I look up at the cold stars overhead, and I realize that tonight, for this moment alone, they are all shining just for me.

To AA and Others Who Helped Me Stop Drinking

by Michelle M. Tokarczyk

When he left
I held myself
so tight I
could not die
though I knew I'd
fall into the night.
I screamed so loud
no pillow could
silence the sound.

Only gulps of scotch
warm a body
so cold.
Only hours of scotch
fill empty
apartments.
Only years of scotch double my body
to a throbbing head;
till I could die.

It is warm
in these basements.
I can last one day
one night
at a time.
The softness
of their triumph
stills my screams.

Believe You Me

by Rita Markley

The first time I saw Yvette she was cracking hard on a piece of gum and shifting her tremendous weight from one ludicrously high-heeled foot to the other. The shoes were obviously new, a shiny burgundy that clashed with the deep copper brown of her skin. She seemed appalled by something; her eyes were flung wide open and staring off into what must have been some astonishing distance. You'd have said she looked like a startled penny. No doubt. And then stared at me with that sharp, expectant grin until I laughed. I watched her closely that whole afternoon, leaning my head from side to side to see between the women who quickly gathered around her. She talked about Carolina summers and rhubarb pie and Chinaberry trees in a voice so loud and thick that it filled the room entirely. One woman, Gloria, interrupted to remind her that she'd spent one summer, just one, in North Carolina and not her whole life. Gloria was standing directly behind Yvette, taller and darker, like one of those impossibly long shadows that stretch away from any shape at the end of the day and make it seem leaner and looser than it could ever be.

"Ain't nobody gonna believe you sat around eating pie neither," Gloria said, "nobody." They laughed loudly together as if that trip south, maybe just the rhubarb, was a very old joke.

The room was crowded by that time. The women who weren't circled around Yvette were standing by the coffee machine, chewing on stir sticks, waving cigarettes and white Styrofoam cups as they talked. They all knew each other. A few of them nodded toward me; one even smiled. You would have acknowledged the greeting, maybe waved, or walked right over to introduce yourself. But I stood at the far end of the room with my back pressed against a filthy window and refused to meet any of those watery done-it-all eyes. The room was drafty and large with brown paint peeling from most of the walls. There were hand-scrawled signs all over the place. Mostly smug little slogans and prayers in day glow reds and greens that turned the whole drab room into a giddy clutter of words and colors.

By the time the meeting began, I'd counted and read all of those signs twice, and I'd watched Yvette so closely that I could tell exactly when she'd shift her enormous weight from one swollen foot to the other. There was a rhythm to it. And a rhythm to the way the speaker for the meeting swayed back and forth as she told us how hard she laughed the night after Len Bias died. She said it seemed like the funniest thing in the world, this big athlete falling right over dead; all that exercise, all those layups, and he couldn't handle a few lines of blow. Lenny, she said, all we heard about that summer was Lenny. Like him dying was some kind of flag, a big red flag. Even the president had something to say about it. Remember? She told us she laughed even harder when they started all that business about saying no. "Like, hey, I'm stealing batteries and pantyhose and sunglasses from the drugstore. Right? Every day. You know, small time. And I'm selling my ass to stinkin' drunk men in the back seat of a rusted out Buick over on Alabama Avenue. I'm doing all that, hey, I'm doing all that nickle and dime for nothing, right, don't need no damn blow, cause all I gotta do is just say no? Come on. Like I'd really rather drive a Buick, wouldn't you? I mean, hey, we laughed ourselves silly over that. God almighty we laughed." She stopped talking for a long time. Her face was covered with sweat and her eyes were so dark and fierce it was impossible to imagine that she'd ever laughed at anything in her life. I wanted to leave, but I thought of you with that idiot grin on your face, and I didn't move. I thought of you on so many summer nights, hollering or laughing at strangers from our front steps. I thought about how you used to introduce me to anyone that passed by as your just desserts or lucky charm.

Depending on the mood. Or the stranger. And I didn't move, not one muscle.

That afternoon meeting was exactly two years ago. I'm thinking about it now, every detail, because it's hard to think of anything else. It was the beginning, sort of. I came back here regularly and gradually moved from the far end of the room to a seat near the front beside Yvette. This week I'm in charge of the folding chairs, arranging them into long straight rows across this bare wooden floor. They're heavy and the metal is cold in my hands so I work quickly, making sure to stack ashtrays at the beginning and end of each aisle. You wouldn't believe how much people smoke in here, talking about excess and then smoking one cigarette after another. The room is already crowded, which means quickly filling with smoke, and I can hear Yvette's voice over all the others. She's telling the group around her about her new VCR, how she can just sit on her couch and be commander of the world with that remote control in her hands.

"Man, I'm telling you," she says, "if you could just have one of those clickers for your kids, you know, fast forward here, now slow it down, hold up, freeze that one there, God we'd have it made."

"What we, Yvette, why you always saying we?" Gloria asks.

"Excuse me, hold on now. I think I hear someone's silly two cents jingling up in the air, about to drop smack in the middle of my conversation... Look, Ms. Wisechild, you gonna tell me how to talk now?" Yvette pulls her bright purple scarf up close around her neck, exaggerating the motion of her shoulders as she makes the adjustment. Then she bursts out laughing and hugs Gloria until that long, lean shadow nearly disappears in her arms.

They carry on like this every week. It's a way to loosen up before the meeting begins, maybe forget for a while the reason they climb those long dingy stairs to this room. I do that too, sometimes. Just forget. But there's always Evelyn, Crazy Evelyn, to remind us exactly why we're here. She is forever telling us all that "de Nile is more than a river in Africa; de Nile is hiding and forgetting and layin' up in you bed when you scared of showing up for life. Gotta show up. At least answer de phone." It's a line from late night television that she's used at every meeting since I first came here. But she tells it to us each time as though it's just occurred to her. Usually it has no context; someone will say she got a new pair of shoes, had the car repaired, bought a case of Coca Cola on sale at the grocery store. And Evelyn will take a deep sigh, then launch down the Nile one more time as though it were her very first trip. No one laughs at her. They say she had some kind of a breakdown one night in Lincoln Park and that it's a miracle she can talk at all. Not even Yvette knows her story. Fortunately, Evelyn doesn't have a clue about what happened either. All I know is that someone, maybe Evelyn herself, sliced the initials C.A.M. so deeply into her left cheek and across her lips that it looks like her whole face is going to break wide open whenever she laughs. You can't imagine an uglier smile.

Just as I finish slamming down the seats of the last few chairs, a woman named Dianne walks over and hands me a cup of coffee. She's been coming to meetings for about a month, just a newcomer.

"Hey, congratulations, you," she says, reaching out to give me a hug with one arm.

"For what? Making so much noise? Remembering the ashtrays, what?"

"Oh quit that, you. Two years, right? Yvette gotta cake."

"And she'll eat most of it herself."

"So."

"So yourself."

"Come on, quit with that. You nervous is all."

"Is that right?"

She flares her nostrils at me as large as quarters and loudly sniffs the air around her. It's an old joke. She wasn't even here when it started. I was the newcomer then, about my third month here, when I suddenly noticed the smell of bleach and detergent wafting up through the windows from the laundromat next door. This seemed remarkable at the time, astounding, because it had been several years since I'd smelled anything at all. I'd lived in a sort of dark half-world with no scent, no vivid colors, no memory to speak of. My body was almost entirely numb to any texture and it was difficult to distinguish one sound from another. An annoying beep startling me at regular intervals might be a truck in reverse or the alarm going off by my bed. Maybe even a truck reversing into my bed. When the phone rang I was never really sure if it was in my apartment or the one next door. You wouldn't believe how many times I jumped up to answer a silent phone. Or ignored the ringing altogether because it got too difficult to decide.

But the time I came here that first afternoon, my nose was so full of clotted blood that I could barely breathe, never mind smell. One at a time my senses had left, single file. You'd probably call it an orderly evacuation and then look sideways at me and roll your eyes. Maybe even tell me not to be such a grim lucky charm. But that's the main reason I came. They can talk all they want in here about losing their children, their jobs, missing this birthday or that Christmas, but what I missed most of all was my own body. It didn't belong to me anymore. And the first sign of it returning, my senses at least, was when I suddenly noticed the bleach and the lemon fabric softeners filling up the whole room. Then I jumped straight up and out of my chair, sat back down, grabbed onto the girl beside me and started jabbering in her ear about Ajax and Lemon Joy and folding fresh washed sheets with you on Sunday nights. I told her how you used to make such a ceremony of doing the laundry, how we folded every sheet like a sacred flag, and how you'd disappear between loads and then return more animated than ever. Lit up. Like a house on fire. "Where's that pouting fruit of my womb?" you'd say, trying to make me giggle, which I did most of the time.

But this girl, it was Gloria, she took hold of both my hands, stared me deep in the eyes, and told me something stupid about bloodhounds and Rip Van Winkle. Then she winked and flared her nose, and we both laughed so hard the entire meeting went silent around us. This made us laugh all the louder and before long everyone was snickering and giggling, slapping thighs and clapping hands like they'd been in on the joke all along. Up and down the rows, women were turning to each other and repeating their own versions of what I'd said:

Is that a sweaty sneaker, a piece of bacon or my neighbors' stinkin' garbage I smell? Lord God Almighty, I know my life's turned around, must be on that high road now, when I can smell my filthy laundry. Yvette's the one who started the hand clapping. She lifted her tremendous bulk up from her throne, anything that woman sits on is a throne, and said it almost made her believe in God, almost, to hear that sour-faced, bony-assed newcomer finally unclench her jaw and let out a laugh that was loud enough to wake the dead.

Her voice is still the loudest in the room. I can hear her telling everyone around her about how she couldn't sit still when she first came here, that she squirmed and wiggled her way through the whole first year of meetings. Like a chubby worm, she says, moving her hand through the air in a twisting wave. She gets like this whenever there's an anniversary. You'd think she was celebrating her own, every single one of them, all over again. Any minute now, she'll start humming "Precious Lord" under her breath, just start swaying back and forth with her hand thrust on her almighty hip, those startled eyes looking up into the heavens, as if she alone can see all the saints, maybe catch a quick glimpse of somebody's God up there, too. You'd surely call her a heavenly penny now.

She sees me looking her way and tries to wave me over to her. I swallow the last of my coffee and nod, keeping my feet firmly in place.

"Come on over here, Ms. Lostchild, time to quit banging those chairs. This the big day, girl. Now get on over here and give me a proper hug." There's no way to refuse. "Who you got coming today?" she whispers in my ear.

"My sister."

"And?"

"Some friends."

"And you gonna punish the rest of us, break our damn ear drums slamming those chairs, 'cause that's all who's coming, right?"

"Don't start, Yvette."

"Start? Did I stop? Good Lord, I must be losing my memory. Seems like I been trying to get you to open your mouth, and wrestle down all that mess for, let me see, what is it? Two years. 720 days exactly, right?"

"I'm here two years, that's what matters, eh?"

"Barely. You barely here at all, baby, believe you me," she says, and smooths the hair back from my face, still trying to see some place way behind my eyes. "Hey, I made a cake, choco-late."

"Bought one."

"Made it with my own damn hands."

"You and Sarah Lee."

"Sarah who? Me and Evelyn made that cake."

"Talk about denial..."

"Talk about de Nile all night. You should of heard her carry on."

We laugh and watch Gloria make her way to the front of the room. She's the chairwoman and signals the start of the meeting by welcoming everyone and reading off a list of announcements. Most of us find seats along the first few rows, scraping chairs, loosening coats, passing ashtrays back and forth as she begins. She asks all newcomers and anniversary guests to respect our traditions and rules. This means they can't tell anyone who they've seen or what they've heard in this room. As if the whole city is banging down the doors to find out. She mispronounces anonymity like she always does and then explains that celebrating an anniversary, no matter what amount of time, is a victory for everyone. A vic-tor-y, she says, with magnificent reverence, as if she's just invented the word and feels deeply pleased saying it aloud for the first time. I start to reach for a cigarette but realize Yvette is holding my hand. She tells me to stop squirming like a child and I tell her to stop fussing like a grandmother. I keep looking up toward the front door, expecting you to stroll into the room, any second now. A fine piece of drama, you'd say. That's why Yvette's so irrita-ble. She sees me looking toward the door and just shakes her head. My anniversary is a reminder that you didn't climb any long dingy stairs to get to a meeting like this one. As if you had a choice. As if everyone can say no whenever they get around to it. Like we'd all really rather ride that Buick. That's why she's annoyed. She's furious that I still talk to you.

Gloria is working herself up to quite a pitch, talking about faith and recovery and parking lot miracles. She sounds like a missionary and she's getting needlessly specific about me too. It's eerie to hear her tell my story as if it were hers to tell, but that's what happens here. We all tell each other's stories. Come on, Gloria, let's hear what it sounds like from those smart chapped lips. She's talking about the bruises, that I was so black and blue those first few weeks that she didn't know what color I was. That my nose bled all the time and my hair was so thin she could see the exact shape of my skull through the strands. Enough. I pull my hand from Yvette's and light a cigarette. She's telling the entire room that she didn't think I was going to make it, not even after I had my first year anniversary. Is that right, Gloria? That she could feel my anger even when I was silent. You'd be rolling and popping your eyes like something electrocuted by now. She hopes I'll find a way to open up this year and let go, to just open up and let go. She sounds like one of those slogans pasted up on the walls.

"She's way out of line," I whisper to Yvette.

"What?"

"She can't stand up there and tell me what I need to do. Not like that."

"She didn't say hardly a word about you. God's sake, she's introducing the speaker is all. Maybe if you stop staring at that door and pay attention you won't be such a nuisance to us all is trying to hear what's going on."

"She's out of line."

"And you're out of your mind. All the way out, believe me. Now sit and listen."

The woman taking Gloria's place at the front of the room looks very frail. Her shoulders are narrow and she has a tiny face with high cheekbones that may have once been pretty. It's hard to tell, though, because her mouth is a dry tight line, almost like a gash above her jaw. But her voice is rich and lilting, and it doesn't seem to belong to her body at all. It's one of those voices that slides right inside you, seeps right into the bones and resonates there even as she pauses. She tells us that it's an honor to be here and that she celebrated her 5th anniversary last month. Then she holds up her hands to us with the palms facing outward and stretches her fingers as far apart as she can spread them.

"I want you newcomers to take a look at your hands. Go on, move the fingers around a little. Look careful, now. These are the hands that lift a drink, ain't they? The hands that load a needle, or grind up a pill. Maybe run a razor blade through a lot of white powder. Go on, now, look at your hands. They nearly killed you, didn't they? You wouldn't be here elsewise, would you? So, understand, you gotta right to be mad with your hands. Let's start with that. Real mad. Be scared of them, too. Look what they done. Go on, look."

Everyone is staring at their hands, not just the newcomers. It looks like a group palm reading or a new kind of meditation. You'd probably laugh and suggest a round of patty cake. Maybe tell them all about how I could never get down the hand motions to Miss Mary Mack. That I'd always forget what to do by the time we got to the silver buttons, buttons, buttons, all down her back. More likely, though, you'd leave the room altogether.

"These are the hands," the speaker continues, "that I saw giving my own child away, handing him right over the hood of a car. Hold him, I said, ain't nobody gonna leave they child with a dealer. Not less they coming right back. Take him, I said, you think I'm not gonna pay. Go on. Nobody gonna leave they baby less they coming right back. Nobody. But I did. One hour blowing, smoking, another hour gone. I can see my hands holding that pipe. See my fingers reaching for a match. It's getting dark by then and I want some more, still don't have my money. Then I remember the baby. It's not my child anymore; it's the baby. You mothers in here know the difference there. Suddenly, that life don't belong to you no more. Like your hands, must belong to someone else. Can't be your own, twisting and reaching like that. Go on, now, look what slipped from those hands. A life, maybe just your own, a hundred Christmas dinners, a Saturday afternoon. You know what slipped through those fingers. And I know, God help me I know, because there ain't anything in this world that breaks quicker than a mother's heart."

She finally pauses that voice, lets it just swell inside us for a while. Yvette is holding my hand again, rocking back and forth and groaning quietly to herself. She's thinking about her own children, everything she missed with them when she was out on the streets or lost in those dark neighborhood bars. That's why she wishes she had a clicker for them, fast forward here, slow it down there. Right, Yvette? That's why she calls most of us child, as if she can somehow gather back her own. Any minute now, she'll tell me that I have to let go of you, that I guard you too close. That's exactly what she says. But that's because her children are all gone. They abandoned her and she's jealous, maybe. But then she'll turn right around the next minute and go on about how she's grateful for being alive, that there's time to forgive and be forgiven. You should hear her go on about forgiveness. Or watch the way she tries to pull you out of me: What happened? Come on, talk to me. How'd she die? How old was she? What color were her eyes, just tell me that, come on, baby, what color were your mother's eyes? When she's feeling generous, she says you had the same disease we all have in here.

"You squeeze my hand any tighter and it's gonna break," she whispers. She wants my attention because she knows I'm thinking about you. That I'm waiting like I always did. "Hey now, easy, let it out easy," she says. "I'm right here, right here with you. Everything'll work out. It's gonna be alright believe you me. It just takes some time. Come on now. I've got you; let it right on out..."

She's whispering in my ear and I can barely hear the speaker. Something about hands again, healing hands this time, strong hands holding on to each other. She sounds like a missionary, a wild-eyed preacher trying to stir up the whole crowd. You'd probably applaud loudly, maybe give her a standing ovation. More likely, though, you'd leave the room altogether. I think about that and lean all the way into Yvette. And then I don't move for a long time. Not one muscle.

Steps

by Cameron Sperry

The piano men grunt and sweat against the weight of the baby grand while I stand at the top of the steps, waiting.

"Almost there," I reassure them, and the black man grunts in answer, I think. He has biceps as big as my thighs, but his muscles are tight, visible beneath mahogany skin, unobscured by excess fat, unlike mine. Bob once called me "piano legs" in front of his friends, years before I knew it was an insult.

There are twelve steps. I know because I count them every time I go out or come in. Twelve is my lucky number. It's the sum of the day, month and year of my birth. An even dozen, whatever that means.

The piano is balanced halfway up the steps. It won't fall because it is tied to the porch railings by thick ropes, which the piano men tighten and secure before straightening their backs. The white man's baseball cap slips off his head and flaps down the steps to the sidewalk, but he doesn't go after it. He wipes his forehead with his hand, pushing his pressed brown hair away from his red-tinged skin.

"Whew!" he says, looking at the hat, which is upside down on the concrete, still swaying from the fall.

The black man reaches his hand into his shirt pocket and shakes a cigarette free. Balancing one palm on the piano, he sticks the cigarette in his mouth, produces a lighter from his pocket, lights the cigarette, and replaces the lighter. The piano sways slightly. Its hind legs hang suspended above the lower steps.

The white man leans one elbow on the piano. I see the muscles in his arm and his jaw work. The piano sways again.

"Come on, man," he says. The black man flicks the cigarette onto the sidewalk near the hat, and the men bend again toward the piano.

Three steps to go. I back toward the door, push it open, stand waiting. The piano men grunt and sweat, heave the piano onto the porch. The black man fishes for another cigarette. The white man goes to retrieve his hat, returns two steps at a time. I cannot do that; my legs are too short. I have to take one step at a time.

Bob was surprised when I called to ask him for the piano. It had been a wedding present to us from his grandparents, who'd sold their house and moved to a condominium too small for the baby grand. Bob had refused to take lessons after the age of nine, but I'd had dreams of the Metropolitan. The piano was what I'd wanted all my life. Bob didn't mind giving it to me.

"Well...sure, I guess you can have it, sure. Uh...wait a minute," I'd heard him speaking to his live-in girlfriend, Roberta. Then he spoke back into the phone. "Sure, you can have it, no problem. Can you get it moved?"

I'd told him I'd hire someone to do it.

"Okay, then. Just let me know when. Are you doing all right?"

I was surprised he'd asked. I hadn't spoken to him since I'd moved out of our apartment six months ago. Our neighbor, Susan, had told me about Roberta one day when she'd come into the office where I work now. Sometimes I caught myself wondering what Roberta looked like, how Bob acted when he was with her.

"Carol? Are you all right?"

Yes, I'd said. Yes, I'm fine. My name is Carol and I'm an alcoholic. And I'm fine. I'm powerless over alcohol and my life has become unmanageable, but I'm fine.

The first time I'd said those words, Bob was sitting in one of the folding metal chairs set up in a Sunday school room watching me as I spoke. He'd talked me into going to the A.A. meetings just to see what I thought. After the first sentence, he'd put his head in his hands, and I stood in front of a crowd of strangers and watched my husband cry. A few weeks later, I'd moved out of our apartment, into this new place.

"Uh, ma'am, you want to get outta the door?" The white man looks at me as he speaks.

"I'm sorry. Here, it goes right in here." I back into the living room, which is empty except for a papasan chair and a dying schefflera bush under the window. The piano will be perfect in here.

"You want it facing the window?" the white man asks, sticking his head through the door to survey the room.

"Yes, that'll be fine." I'm fine. My name is Carol and I am an alcoholic.

When the piano men have positioned the baby grand in the center of the room, I brush my fingers over the keys. I hit middle C and they look at me for a moment, then they go out the front door and down the twelve steps, into their truck.

I think about running through the scales. Instead, I sit in the papasan chair. The black man comes through the door carrying the piano bench. His biceps roll beneath his lustrous skin. I look at the frayed edges of his blue shirt where the sleeves have been cut away, the cloth left to unravel.

"This is a nice piano," he says. "Heavy, too. My upright ain't near so heavy."

I look at him. He runs one large, dark hand over the baby grand.

"I wouldn't mind having one of these, if it wasn't so heavy. I done moved my upright all around this city. Once by myself, that was a job. I reckon you don't move this one too much."

I shake my head. The sunlight coming through the window makes his skin shine like a polished stone. A horn blows in the street.

"I best be going. Take care now."

He goes to the door.

"A piano's a good thing," he says, looking into the street. "It's good company."

He disappears without looking back. I listen to his boots hit each of the twelve steps, listen to the truck drive away.

When the shadows turn into twilight, I move to the piano, rest my unsteady fingers on the cold ivory, and wait in the darkness for a song.

Recovery as an Art

by Marilyn Elain Carmen

Although I have not taken drugs in thirteen years nor taken a drink of alcohol in ten, my recovery from fifteen years of alcohol and drug abuse really began years later. My addiction to pills and booze was a sympton of a much deeper problem, only two of the self-destructive tendencies that I indulged in, so ceasing this behavior as I did cold turkey on my own did not automatically lead me into recovery. Of course, it was no small task to cease deadening my senses with these chemicals. Without that first step, there can be no recovery. I am certain that I would not be alive today had I not stopped when I did.

I started abusing pills and drinking when I was eighteen—aspirins, Compoz, Quiet World, my asthma pills. The drinks varied—rum and coke, slow gin and ginger ale, screwdrivers, whatever I felt like ordering or whatever someone ordered for me at whatever bar. Then as my life worsened, particularly after my first husband left me with two babies and one in my belly, I began my abuse of a myriad of prescription drugs.

It began with my visit to a so-called psychiatric clinic in Harrisburg. I can see the line now as I type the lines of this essay, mostly all women, mostly all minorities, some shabbily dressed, some, like myself, with huge bellies. How thankful I was when the line moved up close enough to the doctor so that I could sit down. My stomach felt heavy, weighted. Finally the nurse called, "Mrs. Roy," and I walked into the small cubicle where the doctor sat. "What's wrong?" he asked. I told him that I was feeling nervous. For some reason I mentioned that my husband had left me with a lot of bills. "Well, that must be what you're nervous about," he advised. I told him something about being used to bills and that was not what was bothering me. I said that I didn't know what was wrong, that I just felt very nervous, anxious. The good doctor then pulled out his little prescription pad and wrote me a prescription for Librium, or was it Valium.

After that it was very simple for me to get these prescriptions refilled or to visit another doctor for a new one. Once I went to a doctor and told him, "I just had a baby, and I'm up a lot at night. I'm having trouble staying awake at work." He gave me a prescription for Dexidrine to keep me awake. How great for me. Pills to wake up. Pills to get me through the day. Pills to put me to sleep. I must have been a walking zombie. It is a mystery to me now how I performed my typing job for the government through all of this.

On days that held no crisis for me, I'd usually take the dosage that was prescribed, maybe just a few more in case I did get upset. Then, when I did get upset about whatever, an eviction notice, notices to appear in court for bounced checks, inability to obtain support for my children from their trifling father, no fuel oil, the electricity being shut off—I'd take a handful of pills and wash them down with whatever I had to drink at the time, be it a glass of orange juice or a bottle of wine. Many times I would take whatever was left in the bottle of pills and sleep parts of my life away. On several occasions, I'd stay in bed for days or even weeks at a time. Every time I'd wake up, I'd reach over and take more pills so I could continue to sleep, getting up only to call in to work sick or feed the children.

Sometimes I would lie limp in bed, unable to move. Once after one of many knock-down, drag-out fights with my third husband, Lyle, I took a number of pills with a bottle of wine. I was lying on our bed with my eyes open, unable to move. I remember him walking into the room. He lifted my arm up, and it fell immediately back on the bed, limp. "Are you all right?" he asked. I must have nodded my head indicating "yes" because he pulled the covers over me and turned and walked out of the room. Damn, a stranger would have at least brought me a cup of coffee or perhaps even called a doctor. I slept it off. That was the one time I was at peace, when I was asleep, which is probably one reason why I took so many pills.

One morning in 1972, after mixing a number of sleeping pills with my morning coffee, I began walking through the living room crying and screaming. Lyle tried to stop me with his usual manner of pushing me around, but I continued to scream. As I write this, I realize I was trying to get some attention from him. I just wanted him to take me in his arms and tell me that everything was all right. I wanted him to talk to me so that I could talk to him. But the son-of-a-bitch just kept pushing me around, yelling things at me like he usually did. "Woman, you must be crazy. Crazy like that woman you call your mother. You'll be dead soon. Just like she was, by the time you are thirty-six." Then he'd start the name-calling. "Ugly. Dumb. Stupid. Tall. Skinny Black nigger." Lyle is darker than I am, but because he is part West Indian, he felt he could call me a nigger.

I continued to scream and thrash around the living room, knocking everything over, vases and ashtrays, plants, everything I could reach. By the time the police that Lyle called arrived, I was completely uncontrollable. They approached me with a straightjacket and somehow tied it around me. You know, the funniest thing is that I knew exactly what I was doing. They thought I was completely out of it, but I could see and feel everything that happened. I believe I was acting out a plea for help, screaming for help, but there was no one to help me. The more I screamed, the tighter they pulled the straps. They thought I was crazy. I certainly was acting as though I were, and I am certain Lyle told them that I was crazy. That was one of his favorite things to tell people, my friends, my family, the police, the doctors, anybody that would listen to him.

I was then taken by the police to a hospital in Plainfield, New Jersey where one of the nurses asked me, after I was quieted from a shot, if I would like to go to the State Mental Hospital for a while. "Why not," I thought. "Maybe someone there will help me." What a joke. Anyway, I was voluntarily committed to Marlboro State Hospital.

During my short stay at Marlboro, I saw a doctor once. As I walked into a small room that was his office, he asked me how I felt. How in the hell did he think I felt being trapped in a place with people screaming all around me, night and day, people sitting in chairs or on the floor oblivious to their surroundings, being herded out of bed in the morning to go make pot holders, eating the garbage they passed off for food, standing in a long long pill line twice a day, and in my case (since I never caused any trouble), being assigned to typing duties, a place where not one damn soul had the sense to ask me to come sit down and tell them what was bothering me. Not that I would have known in those days, but it would have been comforting to have been asked.

"I'm fine," I told the doctor when he inquired about how I was feeling. "I just would like to go home for a visit on the weekend." I had been in the hospital for a week, and I had had quite enough. "Well, Mrs. Carmen, if you can stop crying so much you will be able to go home to visit on the weekend." That was it. I walked out of his office even more confused.

After that, though, I made sure that the nurses never saw me crying, and when Friday arrived they allowed me to go home for a visit, assuming I would return that Sunday. I never returned. Actually, all it took was a phone call from my everloving husband for them to discharge me. Since I had been diagnosed as a neurotic-depressive (or was it a depressive-neurotic), they gave me enough antidepressants to last for a week. Lyle came to pick me up, and as I walked out to the car wearing my fake fur coat and carrying my pills, I wondered if things would be different. I wondered if my cry for help would be heeded, if the name calling and black eyes would cease, if I could talk to this man who I, for some reason unknown to me even now, I had legally married just two weeks prior to my hospital commitment.

Except that I had another type of pill to abuse, otherwise things continued as usual. Pills. Booze. Fights. Black eyes. Pills. Booze. Screams. Bruised knees. Screams. Pills. Booze. My life continued as before even after I found out I was pregnant with my fourth child. God, I was so sick, and I had no idea where to turn for help.

Not long after my baby, Crystall, was born, I started weekly appointments with a therapist at another outpatient psychiatric clinic which was much different than the previous one. After talking to me, she decided that my problem was the way my husband treated me and the children. She suggested that I join a group within the clinic with the goal of building up my self-confidence. I was extremely shy, and afraid to speak if more than one person was in earshot, so the idea of talking in front of many strangers frightened me.

Much to my surprise, I grew to enjoy the group. My mind was so clouded with the drugs that I consumed that I have no recollection of what we discussed. I do know that I kept my drug use a secret; outside of Lyle, no one knew that I abused drugs. Despite my denial, participating opened me up enough to be able to at least speak to others in a coherent fashion.

Something must have clicked for me in that group, because not long after that, I decided to stop taking the pills that I abused for so long. I stopped. Just like that. I was still very miserable and my marriage grew even worse than it had been when I was abusing drugs. I guess Lyle could sense that I was trying to get myself together, and it frightened him. He needed me to be down so that he could feel good about himself. After my marriage continued to deteriorate to the point where I slept with a butcher knife under my pillow, my therapist provided me invaluable assistance that enabled me to leave this abusive man, taking my children with me.

I joined another group, one that dealt with Transactional Analysis. This was also helpful to me because it enabled me to continue to further build my self-confidence. I took only one pill while I was working with this group, and that was to be the last tranquilizer I have taken to this day. I still was feeling very distant from myself, very sick, like I really did not exist. I continued my alcohol abuse, and as my feeling of unrealness increased, so did my drinking. I wondered so many times what was wrong with me.

Continually, I looked to people for help and they always turned out to be the wrong people. I had a number of men friends after the divorce. Although on the outside it might have appeared that I was promiscuous, I was really looking for someone in whom I could confide rather than sex. I was looking for some way to find out who I was. I was searching for a way out of the maze in which I lived. Once I called up a man I was seeing and asking him to visit me because I wanted to talk. When he arrived a few minutes later, nothing I could do would convince him that I only wanted to talk. Interesting how some men feel that everything that evolves between a man and a woman must revolve around sex, and that a woman is not a person, a person who needs to be able to relate to another human being without forever being a sex object. But that is for another essay.

As the years continued to pass, I stopped drinking altogether after realizing I had begun to spend my food money on liquor. The nothingness, the emptiness inside of me also continued. No matter what I was doing, no matter who I was with, it was still the same. I had tried everything I knew, including obtaining three college degrees and doing a lot of extra reading in many subjects. When I was about 33, I found out that I could write poetry, and began publishing my writing. But the emptiness was still there. Most of the time I felt like I was drowning. Nothing could bring me out of that feeling. I'd be up one hour because of a great poetry publication, and by the time the day was over, I'd be in tears, crying over I did not know what.

About six years ago, I started doing extensive reading about Adult Children of Alcoholics, and about two years after that, I joined an ACOA group that met in Iowa where I was pursuing a master's degree in creative writing. It had been a number of years since I was a member of a group, and I felt a little anxious at the onset. We spent a lot of time talking about problems which had no bearing on my life at this time, or ever. I am an American Indian mixed blood woman with a history of three divorces and four children—three of whom were grown. The other members of the group were mostly traditional students, none were minorities. I believe it was very difficult for them to relate to me, perhaps even more than it was for me to relate to them. On the whole, though, my experience with the group was somewhat positive. Right after every meeting, I felt some relief from the dissociation that plagued me. But then by the end of the day, the old emptiness prevailed—the same sensations of drowning.

The group was led by two psychologists, one male and one female. Although I rarely opened up about my own problems, at one particular meeting I decided to speak about how fearful I was feeling. I began to tell the group that I was raised by a schizophrenic mother and aunt. Continuing on with my story, I related that I had witnessed my mother and aunt and cousin attempting to choke my grandmother to death when I was seven years old. Tears rolled from my eyes as I revealed to them how I was told to bring them the butcher knife so they could "finish her off." I had refused.

I must have shocked them because not one person in the group said a word about what I had shared, including the therapists. Perhaps this group's setting was not the proper place to tackle the problems I wrestled with; however, one of the psychologists could have called me aside, asking whether I would like to talk privately. I was asking for help, and again the door was closed before me.

Even so, I continued to attend the group until I left Iowa to move to Philadelphia where I now reside, carrying my emptiness and constant sense of drowning along with my suitcases. I was extremely troubled when I first arrived in the huge and cold city. My furniture and household belongings took over three weeks to arrive due to a mixup with the moving company. In a strange city in a strange house with no typewriter, no books, no pictures, I had absolutely nothing to do except look for employment. The water was rising all around me. I spent many hours crying in my room, only adding to the depth of the river.

I had to find help, so I looked in the telephone book for ACOA meetings and found one that was held at a nearby psychiatric hospital in the lower northeast section of Philadelphia. When I told my adult daughter I was planning to attend the meeting, she was almost horrified. "Mom, there are some places in Philadelphia where you shouldn't go. Can't you find another meeting to go to closer to us?"

"This is the only ACOA meeting in the entire northeast," I told her. And besides, I thought to myself, such things like racial stratification certainly wouldn't apply at such a meeting. There are times when my naïveté surprises even myself.

When I walked into the large room where the meeting was held, I was amazed at the number of people present, at least thirty. As soon as I entered, strange white faces began to stare at me. This really didn't bother me, since I'm not a person who blends in with the crowd. Soon, though, I was to find out their looks were not because they thought I was attractive, but because my skin was not white and my hair was not straight.

I sat next to a woman who glared at me through the entire meeting, her cigarette smoke curling through my long braids and into my asthmatic chest. When I looked over at her, I noticed her hair looked like she hadn't combed it in six months. I continued to sit, though, and listen as person after person rambled on and on about their alcohol-related problems, problems with family members, and so on. Many times I wanted to interject or seek some advice from these people who must have had something to offer to this world other than racial hatred. Each time I raised my hand to speak, the group leader became suddenly blind, so I remained silent the entire time.

About halfway through the meeting, one member started a diatribe about what some Black people who lived on his street had done. I looked in the direction of the leader, hoping he would attempt to negate the speaker's comments, providing some balance and direction for the remainder of the meeting; however, nothing was said about these racist remarks. I, too, said nothing. It wasn't that I was afraid because, unlike the fragile-of-spirit woman who had sat in her first group years before, I had become assertive. Instead, I was in shock, thinking there was no room for racism at a meeting where we were all trying to get well. My daughter, unfortunately, had been correct. Needless to say, I never returned.

"Well," I thought, "that's it. No more groups for me." I believed that I had played out my options for help, and my life continued for many months as it always had, a living Hell. Thank God, I had my poetry, but between poems, between performances, the drowning sensation worsened. Thank God also for my friends who have always provided me with a broad support system. We shared many conversations about children and writing and men.

For years and years, I had prayed every day for God to put

someone in my life with whom I could *really* talk. For all of my adult life, I have searched for someone that I could tell how the sound of that large brown belt with the shiny gold buckle as it whizzed through the air before striking me on my naked child's bones sometimes even now echoes through the air that surrounds my bed in my large room. For all of my adult life, I have searched for someone that I could tell how sometimes when I wake up in the mornings there is no sense of history, no space between the years of my abused childhood and the present, how sometimes I feel that I am still that eleven-year-old child who awakened one cold October to find her mother dead, stiff and cold beside her.

I had tried to talk to my husbands and other men. They either did not take the time to listen, or when they did, they chose to use the information that they gathered against me in the heat of an argument, in order to make me feel even worse about myself. I had tried to talk to my older children until I learned that they too, like their father, were to come to using my vulnerabilities against me when it suited the occasion. I had tried to talk to professionals in the mental health field, and either they only scratched the surface of my problems, or they proved detrimental to my well-being.

I remember once I had written a long letter to a minister who had been friendly with Crystall and me. In October, a difficult time for me because it is the anniversary of my mother's death, I wrote about how sad and afraid I felt, how I went around every day crying. I asked him if he would like to come and have dinner with us and also if I could talk to him about my mother. He did come to dinner, and we talked, but he never mentioned my request to him, and I felt uncomfortable doing so. Perhaps he found my letter unbelievable since I was my usual outward cheerful self. Who knows?

Well, the options were certainly used up as far as I was concerned. Had it not been for my youngest daughter, I really do think I might have drowned. As the months continued in this cold City of Brotherly Love, I felt myself getting sicker and sicker. I could feel the water rushing ever closer to me. I was powerless. Now that my mind was no longer diverted by the confusion that had always been present in my life, be it from drugs, a trifling man, or wondering if I was going to be able to convince a judge not to evict me and my children, the past came flooding in on me.

Without an acceptance letter from a publisher, without a performance where I could lose myself in my words and in the audience, I was becoming completely at the mercy of my childhood, the separation between my past and present becoming quite blurred. The child inside me could find no refuge. She was still constantly at the mercy of my mother, my aunt, and my male cousin who physically, psychologically and sexually abused me for a number of years. There was nowhere left for this child to run. Nowhere left to hide.

"Lord, please send me someone to talk to," my prayer continued as I began to slip more and more inside. I could feel the anxiety building. My right eye would twitch for weeks or months at a time. My dreams were no longer a solace to me, and many times they were very frightening.

Now don't be mistaken, I just didn't sit back and watch myself slip into the water; I was fighting with everything I knew. I did four hours a week of hatha yoga, breathing and meditation. I read a lot, some of which was to enhance my spirituality. I prayed. I wrote more than I have time to type for publication. I took a long, spiritual ritual bath every Sunday, complete with candles, incense, a religious or spiritual book, and classical music. I watched my diet very carefully, and I also used a variety of herbs, vitamins, and food supplements. None of these things, though, were keeping me up out of the water. There just was no connection. No power. I was drowning.

Four years ago, I sought out out the help of yet another mental health professional in desperation. "I feel like I am drowning," I told him. For the first time in my 48 years on this earth, I was able to communicate to another human being exactly how I felt without the fear of being humiliated. For in an instant, I felt as though a heavy weight had been lifted from my soul. This marked the true beginning of my recovery.

The second time I met with my counselor, he told me a story that he said had come to him in a vision. "A little girl was playing in a shallow brook," he said. The child was deaf so she couldn't hear when the dam above the brook broke. The water came flowing down into the brook. When the little girl did become aware of the rising water, she had the opportunity to make one of two choices. One would be to fight the water in an attempt to get away and thereby probably drown. The other choice would be to go with the flow of the water, holding onto a nearby rock if necessary until the brook subsided." In the past few months, I have thought a great deal about the little deaf girl, and have concluded that it was actually the story of my own life, a life filled with the constant fear of drowning.

When I was about seven or eight my schizophrenic mother and aunt put my brother and me in the family car, drove over a bridge that crossed the Susquehanna River and threatened to drive the car into the river if I didn't tell them who told me to be bad. I must have been about seven or eight when these occurrences began. I have no words to express the relief I felt when I finally realized the cause of my fear of drowning, and that with my adult mind I can always reassure the child inside of me the chance of this incident ever recurring is less than none. I am truly out of the water.

Many counseling sessions later, I now spend much time talking about my past with my therapist, which lifts some of its heavy burden from me and allows me a clearer sense of my history. For example, when my mother died, I was not allowed to go to the funeral. My aunt took my brother and me to the movies. Now on a good day, I am very clear on this, and it is just a fleeting thought, however sad. But there are some days when I think about that incident so much, it becomes obsessive. I cry and feel quite sad. The space between the past and the present becomes blurred. After talking about this in a counseling session, I can return this memory to its proper place in my mind. While I know it will travel to the forefront at another time, I am certain, as well, that the intensity is lessened with each recurrence.

One of the very important things I am also beginning to learn is that I have much strength and power within. I have the power to reach inside of myself and take the frightened little child by the hand and lead her away from the water and into the sun. The key to my recovery has been and will continue to be realizing my strengths. I became so used to others belittling me that now sometimes I take over their roles—perhaps the familiarity is even comfortable, no matter how miserable it makes me. When I learn to really believe that I am a strong, good person, I will be able to stop beating up on myself, and maybe even stop demanding so much of myself.

I know I am getting there. The drowning sensation is almost completely gone. For the first time in my life, I am free of my past several days during the week. The big brown belt does not come out as much these days. Nor am I as haunted by my mother as I've been in the past. The child inside of me is waking up, and I am getting in touch with her. I allow her to play more. It is okay to laugh. It is okay to have fun. I am learning to tell jokes or sing without the fear of someone slapping me, and I can look in the mirror and see that I am not ugly.

As I learn to make space for the child inside of me to live, in a sense, I am giving myself back my childhood. My bedroom contains a desk scattered with papers and books and a typewriter. Certificates and degrees hang on one all. On the other side of the room are families of stuffed animals—rabbits, cats, dogs, bears, owls. On that wall hang photos of two of my childhood idols, Gary Cooper and Gene Autry. Then there are family pictures, poems and inspirational quotes. I even have some jacks and marbles on my dresser. Balloons hang in a corner by the window, and a Little Golden Book that Crystall gave me for Christmas sits on top of my bookcase.

There are times when I wake up in the cheerful room that I have just described and break into a fit of fearful tears, wondering how I can make it through the day. But I always do make it, and that is what is important.

Waves

by Valerie McMillan

When other people look at my résumé, they are almost always impressed by my list of accomplishments. When I look at it, there are only two things I am truly proud of—working on a foundation that builds bike trails and getting my master's degree. The rest were performed by a human doing, not a human being—a human doing who had learned to compulsively use drugs, alcohol, work and sex to numb me from having any feelings other than occasional rage or temper tantrum.

As a young girl and teenager I had been sexually abused by a male babysitter and by my dad. Being raised Catholic in a dysfunctional family was a double bind. Our family had to look good to the outside world while chaos reigned at home. If I didn't maintain a good-girl image, I would bring shame on the family. When I finally told a priest what was happening, he advised me to tell my father to stop...easy for an unmarried priest to say.

As I moved into adolescence and became aware of the pleasurable sensations my body was capable of producing, I grew even more confused. When my father began to force himself on me, I hated the way my body would betray me by responding, so I learned to crawl into my mind until the entire event was over. Now all my friends could talk about was boys and dates. I had mixed feelings. I liked guys, but they always seemed to want sex like my babysitter and father had or to use me in some other way. Emotional and physical intimacy were terrifying prospects.

On my eighteenth birthday, I discovered what seemed like the perfect solution—beer. I honestly didn't like the taste, but

I really liked the numbing effect it had on my mind. I couldn't think or feel if I drank. Finally I knew I could find inner peace or at least what I believed was inner peace.

In college I found that drinking was not only acceptable, but encouraged. People got attention for how bombed they were at a party. One night I got totally blitzed and tried to play Peter Pan down the stairs in the dorm. I hit my head, got a concussion and ended up in the hospital for four weeks. As soon as I was released, I went back to drinking.

By the second semester of my freshman year, I had a nervous breakdown and my psychiatrist prescribed Valium and Dexamil. He also told me all I needed was a good lay. After that I mixed alcohol and drugs regularly, ending up in the hospital once more because of an overdose. I lost forty-five pounds, learned to smoke and keep most of my escapades private. I had to keep up the good-girl image, even though I would drink and drug myself into oblivion at college and come home and be the perfect daughter.

When I graduated, my parents had a brunch at the Ramada Inn for my friends. We looked like the perfect family—all we needed was for Beaver to walk in the door and ask for a snack. After my parents took the obligatory pictures showing how happy we all were and left, I began my own party. Neighbors had given me ten sample liquor bottles—tequila, scotch, bourbon... I decided to drink all of them. After all, it was my graduation and I needed a little pick-me-up. My brother, who had stayed to move me back home, ended up driving me to my parents' house. I helped him drive by throwing the car into neutral a few times.

Little did I know my folks had planned a surprise open house for me and invited all their friends to meet the new college graduate. It was their way of showing off what a good family we had. If I looked good, they looked good. Needless to say, they weren't impressed when I fell out of the car and threw my diploma at them, saying, "Here's your fucking degree." I went downstairs and changed clothes, all the while ignoring their pleadings to at least say hello to the guests. Then I disappeared with an old boyfriend until three in the morning.

From that point on, I grabbed any opportunity to numb

out. My career as a teacher began with one hell of a party, and I continued to party every weekend. Numbing out became a way of life with any change or transition. Weddings, funerals, graduations, holidays, birthdays, weekends, Mondays, a good day at work, a bad day at work, you name it and I could rationalize a way to party.

Eventually, I became two different people—the daytime educator and the nighttime party girl. When I was the party girl, I could be intimate with men. Now when men wanted intimacy, I would just drink more, numb out, and put out. I became a tease and often put myself into compromising and even dangerous situations. One time, I remember being so drunk at a sleazy bar that my date was trying to have sex with me in the booth in front of a lot of drunk patrons. We finally left half-clothed and continued in his car.

My relationships deteriorated until all that was left were drinking buddies who would party with me. If I got smashed enough we would have sex. Sometimes I would wake up with people I didn't even remember meeting. Pretty soon it didn't matter what we did as long as I was numb. I liked the attention at the time and didn't mind the sex if I had enough to drink. Sex had become as much a mood-altering and numbing escape as chemicals.

My mother died when I was twenty-five. To stuff the pain of her death, I began a very hectic, kinetic lifestyle, sleeping only four or five hours a night. Teaching tennis and catechism, working full time, competing in tennis and racket ball, drinking every night to pass out and catch a few hours of "sleep," helped me to stuff my feelings so deeply inside that I didn't realize how much her death had affected me until nineteen years later when I finally stopped drinking. I also turned to politics as a way to self-medicate my pain.

I was thirty-two when I was elected to city council and became vice mayor. Finally, I thought, this would be the perfect opportunity for me to clean up my act and become really respectable. I knew I wasn't one of those bums in the gutter. The last thing I wanted was to be found out. For a while I was able to keep up the "good" image and not over-drink or get into compromising situations. Then things began to fall apart. I *had* to drink to attend functions. Without a few drinks, I was nothing. After a few drinks, I was the life of the party. I would attend conferences out of town alone as a representative of the city, attend open houses, get smashed, get laid, and wake up with someone I didn't remember meeting, much less his name.

Some of my colleagues started to catch on to my game, but even so I continued to drink, and the drinking moved closer to home. I found a neighborhood bar where I could stop by for a "few" after work. After three or four hours I would drive home, call a man and either meet him or he would come over. We would have sex and pass out. I hated the next morning and was often late for work.

I really was doing the double life stuff again, and I couldn't stop. I thought I could handle my drinking, but I couldn't—it was handling me. My drinking had become insatiable and so did my need to be the center of attention and get all the recognition I could. Inside I felt empty and worthless without my alcohol.

By this time I was a school counselor. I would run Children of Alcoholics groups while I had a hangover. I always looked good (my family had taught me to look good), but emotionally I was as distant to those children as their parents. Usually my mind was on what had happened the night before and who I would party with next. Once I was even sleeping with a student's father. After all, we were drinking buddies. How could I help other people while I was still in my addictions and denial?

I hit the wall at the age of forty-four. Suddenly drinking and drugging didn't numb me out anymore. I was sleeping until 1:30 am and waking up with night terrors. It took more and more to stop my mind from working overtime. I started therapy to deal with the past sexual abuse and other issues.

Chest pains put me in the hospital for four days. I was told to either change my habits or I would die. My days of sleeping with Dionysus were over. I cut back my work schedule for the rest of the year and focused on stopping smoking, drinking and drugging.

My recovery has been slow. I work on it every day, one day at a time and one step at a time. Some days are easy and some knock me off my feet. It's been like walking on the shoreline. Sometimes the waves lap at your feet and you can keep walking. Once in a while a bigger wave hits you and the walk gets tougher. If you try to run, a huge wave comes along and you are forced to walk once again.

The slow process of getting reacquainted with myself and learning to feel my feelings rather than numb them with alcohol, drugs, sex and work, has been like finding a long-lost friend, someone I used to know inside and out, but lost along the way. Sometimes I can look her face to face in the mirror and smile. Sometimes I even wink.

Next Time

by Lisa Martinovic

my friend said
she wanted to remember
next time
that her heart is attached to her vagina
Sounds painful

I wondered how attached *are* they
AND
how are they attached

is it with a long linkage of old rubber bands
the kind used on newspapers
so that the vagina might have some choice as to
how far she could stray before reaching the end
of heart's tension
and boinging
back up against a startled aorta or ventricle?
ouch!

or is it with steel cabling
from a shipyard
no give here,
both ends bolted into flesh with
iron nuts

perhaps the heart holds her partner at the end of a long leash
periodically unfastening so that the unfettered vagina
can romp merrily through penisland without attachment?
I usta think so

are they connected with string,
tin cans at either end
two kids on the original intercom system
Heart to Vagina, do you read me?
Heart to Vagina, proceed at your own risk
if you go any deeper I'll be swallowed up with you

maybe heart and vagina are bonded
through their very own private umbilical cord
pulsing messages and nourishment
back and forth
in and out

I think my friend is right
I also want to remember
next time
that my heart is attached to my vagina

and maybe
next time
I'll let my heart go first

Sex: Then and Now

by Anne Stirling Hastings, Ph.D.

Long before uncovering my healthy sexual self, I was in a marriage where I hated sex. Years of psychotherapy hadn't given me a solution. I absolutely hated it, even though Richard was a nice man and seemed to be a good lover. He was enormously attracted to me, touched me gently and always wanted me to have an orgasm. From the beginning, Richard had hovered over me, wanting sex every moment I was willing. I dreamed at night I had to keep him alive by holding his heart to prevent it from falling out, leaving only one hand for the rest of my tasks of living. It was difficult for me to desire sex with a man who attributed so much meaning to it.

I particularly remember one afternoon when a man who worked in my favorite grocery store asked me for a date. He was married, but ready to leave his wife, and he thought I was separated because I had stopped wearing my wedding ring a few weeks earlier. He had been embarrassed, and we both blushed, but I was flattered. That evening, after three days without sex, Richard needed his fix. I had a difficult time getting aroused, but the memory of my grocery store encounter sparked a little sexual interest for me, just enough to prepare to meet my marital requirement. I poured a glass of wine so I wouldn't gag when I told him I was ready. The blessed alcohol made me feel sexual so that I could override my discomfort—my rage, actually. I gulped the wine as I bathed and, feeling ashamed, I rubbed my clitoris to make sure I would stay aroused.

As we climbed into bed, I wished I had drunk more of the wine, but I knew I couldn't reach for my glass. Part of my script required being immensely responsive to his touch, so drinking while with him would mean I was more interested in the wine than in him—a truth I wasn't ready to face.

We went through the steps in order—kissing, breast stimulation, oral sex. To reach orgasm, I thought again of the man in the store, imagining his hard penis next to me. Knowing sex with him wasn't possible because we were both married, was arousing. I slipped over the edge, and the orgasm grabbed me up, squeezed tightly, then dropped me roughly on the bed. It was over. I was grateful the other man's interest enabled me to have sex with my husband. Without wine and fantasy, I would have to leave Richard.

Years later I did leave, in April as the days were becoming long, and summer was on its way. When we moved a new bed to my clean, fresh apartment, Richard suggested we initiate it. I tried to hold back my disgust as I told him no. He didn't seem to understand that I was starting a new life that included no more sex with him.

The change proved to be frightening and lonely as well as exciting. Thinking that Richard had been the sole reason for my lack of desire, I set out to date many men—without wanting a committed relationship. My search seemed to give me purpose, and certainly it occupied my time and emotions. I didn't understand that I was using sexual energy addictively. I also didn't know that my lifelong use of sexual fantasy was really an addiction designed to make an empty life seem full. I didn't fully understand healthy sex until years later when I wrote a book about it, teaching myself as I went, while practicing with my second husband.

By June, I'd had sex with two men. Both lived in other states. I was intrigued by the possibility of having several lovers, enjoying sex without entanglements. Those brief encounters made my strategy seem to work because a few days or even a few weeks weren't sufficient to create ties that I would have to break. During that time I always slept alone in my own bed so I could put my hands over both edges to prove to my body that no one was there needing me. I was free. No man could control me. Then I met Greg.

He was my landlord and lived in the mirror-image apartment next to mine. His wife lived in another state, which allowed me to believe he was free, but in truth they weren't separated. I didn't know he was a sex addict too, an affair addict, who'd engaged in extramarital sex almost from the beginning of his 25-year marriage.

When he invited me out to lunch, I filled him in on my philosophy of having sex with a number of men without hurting anyone. He soon expressed interest in being one of those men, and laced it with romance, flattering me in ways that felt loving and real. Every morning when I stepped out my door for my newspaper, a note was inside it or tacked to the wall. Every evening he called to see if I wanted to do something, delighted when I said yes. Grand Marnier in cut crystal brandy glasses became part of our pre-sex ritual, a touch of elegance supporting the illusion that this was wonderfully special. At last I had the man who would make up for every bad thing that happened when I was a child! My daddy loved me. Within a few weeks I fell in love with him, became monogamous, and wanted to couple. In truth, I was fucking another woman's husband.

Three months after the beginning of our affair, Greg went to visit his wife, Linda, planning to tell her about our relationship. She fought to save their marriage, and immediately moved to be with him. He, at last, felt wanted. Her presence in the apartment next to mine made my behavior vividly clear. Hearing their noises next door, I mourned him and pitied her. My pain was excruciating. Every time I opened my front door, I wondered if I would see her. When I did, the silence hurt.

After two weeks, I asked her to speak with me, and she agreed. We drove and talked for two hours. I learned that she'd created her life around this man for twenty-five years until they lived apart. He'd gone to California for work and she had planned to sell their house and follow. But much like me, she found it freeing to establish herself as a separate person, no longer under his shadow. Now she blamed herself for his affair with me.

Afterwards I contacted a friend who could listen as I yelled passionately that I would never again be with another woman's husband. The accompanying sobs pulled out pain from deep within my body and were cleansing. At the time I wasn't aware that as a small child, I'd had sex with my mother's husband—my father. Although our culture said that couples have sex only with each other and not with others, that wasn't how I'd grown up. Now I could see that couples deserved to have boundaries around their sexual loving, excluding all others, especially their children.

Greg tried to resume contact with me after we broke up, but it was too painful, and perpetuated our dependency. I stopped him from calling, hoping I could grieve more quickly, but I didn't finish that process. Instead, I immediately set out to find another man to replace him, one to get me through the winter. The search only took four weeks, but it felt interminable.

I met Randy at a party. He was much younger than I, and wanted to have children at some point, so he wasn't an appropriate mate. I assumed this made him safe because it would prevent me from bonding to him in the way I had with Greg. Yet within weeks we were tightly woven into a monogamous relationship. I became jealous and possessive, and he moved into my apartment. As I transferred my addiction to Randy, the pain from losing Greg soon ended, replaced by the pain of yet another relationship addiction.

The fact that Randy left drinks untouched or half-full, forced me to take a look at my relationship to alcohol . My friends and lovers had always drunk more than I did. Since I had a low tolerance and would drink one or two glasses of wine while others drank many, I considered myself a light or social drinker. Because Randy didn't join me, I began to notice when I wanted alcohol and why. I drank every evening after work while making dinner to "unwind." I drank for the aphrodisiac effect even when I desired sex, believing I couldn't maintain arousal if I abstained. Now I continued to drink, but I wasn't comfortable with it.

Six months after meeting him, I treated Randy to the birthday dinner he'd requested at an expensive restaurant. As he ordered the steak and lobster, and I felt powerless to set limits on how much I was willing to spend, my feelings simmered. He drank with me that night, large glasses of wine that affected us during the long periods between ordering, salads, and finally the entree. Before our coffee arrived, we were sending tense sentences across the table, and holding back feelings with no real understanding of what was occurring.

As Randy and I slept on opposite sides of the bed that night, I was struck with the awareness that alcohol had prevented me from knowing what was going on. I wanted to vomit it up, strip it from my brain, and refuse to allow it to remove my feelings. From that time on, I stopped drinking, no longer willing to tolerate the confusion and pain that accompanied substance-induced blindness. Finally I was willing to face life without my aphrodisiac.

Within a few months the relationship ended. Alone in my little house, I made a commitment to myself—I would not search for a man, and remain celibate for at least one year. I could see at last that pain caused by addiction was as bad as pain from deprivation. Intuitively, I sensed that my only hope was going through my loneliness and despair to find a new place. It wasn't easy.

I could tolerate being home alone for a night, only if I had a roaring fire going all evening and if I talked to at least one person on the phone. Two evenings alone were too much. Yet when I was with people, I didn't feel connected. Work was a blessing because it resembled life prior to swimming in a sea of loneliness, but I dreaded weekends. I saved my health and curbed my depression by playing racquet ball several hours a week, but that wasn't why I did it. The total distraction of a vigorous sport eased my pain.

During this time, my first memory of my father having sex with me surfaced. I also remembered my mother's hatred of me for what he did. Apparently living out my addiction to men had prevented such memories from emerging, but once I was entirely exposed and vulnerable, I had no defenses to prevent them from rising to the surface. Without quite understanding consciously yet that I was an incest survivor, I benefited from exploring and respecting these memories. Now my previous destructive involvement with a married man made sense.

Six months later, while walking through a shopping mall, the feeling of being in love swept through me. There was no man in my life, and I marveled at how this sensation wasn't connected with a sexual relationship—it came completely from within. This new understanding of being loved helped set me free.

Both my celibacy and work with childhood memories changed my views of partnering. I wanted to explore the uncharted world of healthy loving rather than compulsive bonding. After fifteen months of celibacy, I met a man whose sensitivity and commitment to inner growth attracted me. With little working understanding of healthy relating, and without feeling any need to have a partner, I decided to interact with him to see what would happen.

Mark came to my house the night after the workshop ended, and we talked about our respective work on relationships. He was distraught over his recent separation, but was also looking forward to a new life. I knew he wasn't ready for partnership, but we decided to have sex anyway. He said that he felt affirmed by my attraction to him, that it countered years of his wife's anger.

The sex we had felt physically satisfying, and for several nights afterward, I was relieved that my addiction was abating—I hadn't fallen in love. Within two months, however, things began to change. I started feeling closer to this man even though I could see that he wasn't a suitable mate because of his recent divorce and because he didn't share my approach to life. When he planned to refinish the cabinets in his kitchen I wanted to help, ready to nest with him. I liked him, I liked having sex with him, and no other relationship pulled either of us away, but I awoke one morning knowing I had to stop sleeping with him. Puzzled over this, I wrote pages and pages in my journal trying to explain it to myself. Finally I realized that lovemaking, at least for me, was for bonding into a partnership. Mark and I weren't ready to do that.

After we stopped seeing each other, my alone time and time with friends was more fulfilling than before. Six more months passed as I immersed myself in my work, played racquetball and coordinated a conference on men's issues. Celibacy and self-love took me through the summer and into the fall, when I met Rex. By this time I was content to be without a man, and was planning a move to another state. Shorter than I am, clean-shaven, and with gray hair he wasn't the type my addict self was attracted to.

Because of this, I gave no thought to the possibility of him as a lover. I didn't look like his stereotypical mate either, but we quickly grew to be friends and eventually lovers. So began a tumultuous relationship, filled with anger, shame and deep honesty—along with freely flowing sex that followed no order either of us had ever known.

Rex became catatonic with shame that originated in his childhood, and I felt desperate urges to throw him out of my life. But we talked and felt and talked some more. Each Friday we moaned over the impending weekend of struggle and love, knowing we would emerge Monday morning changed. And Monday brought the relief of returning to normal life back at work, both eager for and frightened of the next Friday. We were able to persist when things seemed so chaotic that we thought we couldn't stand it.

Now six years later, we are settled into a solid, smoothly working marriage. We skilfully resolve conflicts. Retrieval of childhood memories has become a way of life for both of us, sort of interesting if it weren't for the accompanying pain and disorientation. Our sex is both wonderful and frightening as we grow closer each year.

We arose early today because the sun was shining in our window, enticing us to awake on our day off. As we stood at the end of our bed after pulling the covers into place, I saw myself reflected in his adorable, child-like face. He looked like how I felt. We hugged and I was aware of the bulge of my stomach pressed against his, the soft friendliness of bodies long acquainted, each fold accustomed to the fit. As my breasts and vulva ignited with sexual energy, I felt his penis growing against me. With the morning open before us, we could allow our bodies to take over.

We carried our sexual hum to the shower, soaping ourselves and each other, touching our plump roundness. With twenty-five more pounds than when I was thirty, I adore my body. Every square inch of both of us is the flesh we get to love each other in. The thought of drinking wine didn't cross my mind. From years together, I know that freely flowing sex is possible only without it.

After we dried ourselves, we returned to bed to see what will happen next. Giggling like kids, we patted and stroked, until the next thing to do became clear. Rex lay down and I lay on top of him while he touched my breasts, creating waves of sexual arousal that filled my chest and streamed down through my pelvis. I held his semi-erect penis snugly against my waiting vagina. Our bodies talked to each other. My vulva lubricated, his penis grew hard. As it slid inside of me, a wave of sparkling exuberance flooded up my body and out, over Rex. His flooded over me, too.

The swirling, electric arousal grew as I moved. Each cell in my vagina seemed to vibrate, and the energy flowed in different patterns within me and between us. We laughed again as our bodies swelled and molded to each other. I looked into his eyes, drawing him into me as I watched his skin change and his breath expand. As we moved and moved, our bodies approached orgasm and then dropped back in unison. It wasn't time to be finished; we wanted more.

We rolled over, Rex on top now, and I put my legs down to feel the pull on my clitoris, the pressure of his legs moving against my inner thighs. All soft and plump, I felt formless and weightless. I felt like we had been doing this for a very long time, but I wasn't sure because I didn't look at the clock.

Then my arousal vanished. I startled slightly as I saw that intercourse was over. As I looked at Rex to tell him, he smiled at me. "My penis is going down," he said softly. "And your arousal is gone, isn't it?"

"Yes," I told him, still amazed that our bodies were able to decide these things, communicate them to each other and respond accordingly. Sometimes we can figure out why they have decided to take a certain course, but at other times, it doesn't make much sense. Our bodies understand what our brains don't. If we force arousal to continue or fuel it with alcohol or fantasy, we lose each other—sometimes for hours. Instead, this morning we embraced, smiling, and our conversation turned to the day ahead.

Reclaiming the
Goddess Within

Into the Roar

by Ruth Shaer

The edge of a beginning.
That moment at the end of an exhale,
That moment,

                suspended
when there's nothing to do
except
be
in the void
and wait.

Being is not something they teach at school.
It comes before action
so you are smooth
even when your path isn't.

Being so you can learn
to recognize your
trul soul nature
without covering up
with the smiles of addiction
and hugs that don't touch.

Being is feeling your feet on the ground—
your arches and toes and heels,
lying on the sand,
allowing the particles
to mold to your body
like a sculptor draping you in clay.

Being is curling into your foetal pain,
embracing it
without killing yourself,
crying
without wiping away your tears
letting the rivulets meet under your chin
like the bow of a baby's bonnet.

Being is switching off the video of illusion,
marching in place
for as long as necessary,
despite your terror,
until you're ready to open
the mouth of the lion
and put your hand inside,
lovingly,
with compassion. And that moment
when you think the lion will kill you,
instead,
she licks your hand
with her large red tongue.

The Bear

by Hilary Mullins

This is about the bear. I must tell all of you about the bear. Even though now, tonight, she seems far away from this place - this hall, with its lights and the scraping sounds of chairs. But she is here. She is here with me, with you, with us, now.

I did not always remember this. There were years I forgot her, buried what before I had always known. Then came the night she took me back, a night that fell fast, a dusk thick with stirrings, the tops of trees twisting in the wind. A night just like this one, in fact—the kind to bring you wholly back to yourself as only night can.

Imagine, it was already late as I started out to the horse shed, a sloshing water bucket bowing me to one side. I crossed the road and the horse, my dark-maned mare, was wheeling in high-hooved circles in her small pasture. Anxious, she gave a few frightened kicks towards the sky thickening with clouds.

I thought at first it was the wind unsettling her as a gust lifted my hair, laying its long insistent hand against my back. I was not surprised at the force of it—the season was the very last of fall, the time of year when weather reasserts itself as an actual force in your life. There is much to be said for a thing that shakes us and will not be denied: a blizzard, a hurricane, an earthquake. And yes, even love. Oh, especially love.

That is why the bear came back. I had slipped into the comfort amnesia brings. I think you know the sleepy, silencing arms I mean. So, at first she was just a dark shape the other side of the fence. I almost could have missed her. Do you hear me? I almost could have missed her. Where would I be now if I had? But no matter. I saw her. She was there; she was with me.

I gave the horse her water, her grain and hay. I put her in for the night and stepped back out into the dusk. The bear was still there, waiting. I knew she would be, and suddenly I was aware she had been waiting for quite some time.

I stood along the dirt road that runs by my house and looked over at the massive, thick shape. I seemed to think her eyes were yellow and that she was looking straight back at me. Then I heard her shifting her great weight, saw her turn and start her shambling way up the tree-covered mountain that rears toward the horizon over my homestead.

I was afraid, afraid because I knew she meant me to follow her. And I also knew, fast and hard and for the first time, that was why I had refused to bring her into sight for so long. You must understand this—my fear was great—it was greater than I was for a long time. The wind lifted, pressed against my back, urging me. I could stay and live on in a state I vaguely recognized as half-submerged, or I could set off now after her, toward what I knew not, some new way of breathing, perhaps, some way of bursting to a surface beyond the strange muting that hazed over my life, smothering my days.

I flung the empty water bucket and tore after her, over the fence and up that steepness filled in with saplings and bushes, old stumps and pricker vines that sunk their many-pointed sharpness into my coat and hands. Up, up. Up, up. I could hear her, wading through the underbrush, a moving occasion of branches breaking and the dragging sounds of old growth giving way. Myself, I do not know how I could have moved as fast toward the brim of the hill as I did, but she was moving even faster. And when she arrived there, ahead of me, she must have stopped, for suddenly I heard nothing save the rasping of my own strained lungs.

Nothing. I tore on faster still. But when I burst into the meadow that encircles the mountain top, I could see nothing, just the long-tipped grasses bending in the wind and the first few frosty stars in the purple-blue sky overhead. Nothing! I circled around and around, spun in smaller and smaller circles until I was clutching myself in a dizzy orbit that sent me plunging to the ground.

Not there, not there. She was not there. I had come all this way and she would not wait. I would never find her now in this night. Huge as the night is, there is nothing larger than the night, not even the ocean. She would have slipped back to her cave under cover of darkness, and winter was creeping up the hill on its long, icy fingers. I would be overtaken and all alone. Starvation is a worse thing than sleep, and I had been cold and hungry all my life. I had been brought to the bare top of the mountain and left there to die.

I dug my fingernails into the earth then and wailed, a bawl as deep and wild as any cub's, wailed for all that I had ever wanted and lost, a cry of outrage that I could have been brought this far and not taken through.

And so, yes, she appeared, suddenly, enormously, a cavernous looming over me, a mammoth bear reared mountain-like on hind legs, her mouth grimacing and out of it, the sound of a thousand thousand forests gnashing in high wind.

I may have screamed. Perhaps I even died. It's hard telling. But still, it was the only thing—this bulk out of the earth, this seizing of me in my very bones, the way she scooped me up into her huge and furred folds, wholly embraced me in the heart of her great bear body, the utter warmth and smell of her. No noise now.

She carried me, tucked within, to a dent in the hill, a place that went down and in, a bed of leaves. Outside the snow began to fall. I had no clothes left now, peeled away to skin. She started a soft, scratchy licking of my length, layers shedding, settling in amongst leaves, earth, scraps of fur and bone, until my eyes closed and I was pink and new, sinking like any newborn into a mother's offering side.

That was all. It was not that I grew the tufted hair of an animal, but that I traveled up into a new kind of sleep where dreams were once again possibilities and fire could not only be entered but embraced entirely. Outside the snow was falling fast. I slept, dreaming my way all through that first winter night of the year. And when I awoke in the morning under a pile of leaves and fir branches, I knew she was gone, but that she had left me with myself.

I drew back on the leggings, the wool sweater and jacket, the thick boots. And as I emerged from that small holding place in the mountainside, I knew she had been there all those years, spiriting my dreams from out of the air where they had slipped away from me below in bound sleep. I knew she had stored them in the generous fat and maw of her great bear self until I was ready for her to offer them back to me. And now, returned, they finally were mine.

Mine that morning as I stumbled out, blinking like a baby in the brilliance of the sun, into a world softened with snow, holding in my hands these dreams of a life with women, of a life that cannot be surrendered but must be reclaimed day by day, again and again fought for and won. A life, too, to be savored, lived in nerves that sing with quickening and love. Those were the dreams she'd given me back in the night, transmitted in the gritty gentleness of her tongue across my skin, over and over reminding me till finally I was a body once more awake to herself. I thanked the bear that morning, shouted out on the frosty air to her presence and took off back down the hill, headed home.

The Healing Circle

by Patricia Heyne

The soul of my healing floated in the ethers of my psyche for five years. Her conception occurred one night in a dream. What would it be like to be free? Her gestation was painful and long with much false labor. The agony of her birth nearly took my life.

When her newborn mouth touched my breasts she found them empty and void of nurture. I, like a mother bird who senses human touch on her chicks, pushed her out of the nest. But my newfound sobriety landed by the grace of the Great Mother in the arms of a foster mother whose breasts were full. She watched over and fed the young soul of my sobriety tediously, for this infant cried much at first. In the circle of her love, my sobriety lived.

This adoptive mother's name is Anonymous. She runs her house and store by a set of twelve rules that set me free. Her nature is spirituality. Her milk is forgiveness. Her love is a ring of commitment to the health and well-being of her children who link hand-in-hand to keep her strong.

The baby suckled long in this circle of love. She grew into a toddler whose first steps alone caused her the pain of separation anxiety. But each faltering step was righted by the care and compassion of the Lady of the Circle and the Great Mother, the One Who Knows.

In the care of the Great Mother, this baby thrived as she passed through all the stages of development. Her childhood brought curiosity, exploration and skinned knees. Her adolescence brought an inner battleground of insecurity. Along the way, many times she felt the cold, dead breath of the one left behind chill the back of her neck. If it were not for the loving hands of the circle, the vampire would have pushed the coffin lid open and sunk his long, yellow fangs into the tender flesh of this neophyte every time the sun went down.

And what of my sobriety now? She is a woman in full bloom. Her life is a treasury of delicate flowers, snowflakes and poetry. She is foster mother now to the new infants whose hunger has not yet been satisfied. She is a keeper of the circle and a lover of the light. She is guardian of the powers that keep her free. Her serenity, courage, and wisdom are blazing torches in a world once filled with darkness. She sings of creativity and from her flows a river of gratitude that washes her days new, one day at a time.

She knows now she may send heavenward the burning arrows of her faith and in return drink from a golden goblet with crystal contents that are never bitter, and the goblet always runneth over. Her new names are Life and Acceptance. Her sisters are the white light of love and the red blood of pain. She no longer pushes a river but is continuously nourished by a soft glow from within.

Sweet Thing and Wild Thing:
a fairy tale of addiction and recovery

by Alice Bolstridge

In the beginning, there was only one. And in that one, life got too big for itself and burst apart into two. It was felt as a very big pain in the womb. And especially the one who became two felt one very big pain, which quickly was two big pains. And so two were born instead of one in a very big and very old house. The birth of those two changed everything forever.

First one was born with a soft, gentle cry. She smelled like sweet hay in the field, and the parents said, "Goodness! what a sweet thing," and smiled in gladness. Then one was born with a loud roar. He smelled, right away, like a barn invaded by a wild creature. And the parents said, "Goodness, what a wild thing," and frowned in worry and disappointment. And so they were named: Sweet Thing, Wild Thing.

Sweet Thing pleased her parents in every way. When she wanted attention, she cried softly, sometimes so softly that no one heard her: the parents were busy running the house and farm and throwing parties for all the countryside. Keeping up appearances. But Wild Thing roared when he wanted attention, and got whacked, which made him roar louder. Sweet Thing trembled in fear to hear her brother roar and to see him get whacked.

So they grew.

Sweet Thing grew sweeter and sweeter in fear and trembling. Her smile grew wider and wider. Sometimes she lay unnoticed in her bed for days, whimpering softly.

Wild Thing grew wilder and wilder in terrible anger. He grew horns on his head, and fire flamed from his eyes. He grew teeth he loved to bare in a wicked grin. Soon he turned and whacked Sweet Thing every time he was whacked.

Sweet Thing grew terribly afraid and ran away from him whenever she could. But one day he cornered her and she could not run away. She did the only thing she knew how to do. She grew sweeter. She reached out and hugged Wild Thing and kissed him on the mouth.

Then Wild Thing did an astonishing thing. He hugged her back, and kissed her, and picked her up in his arms and carried her to the bed where they lay down together. He murmured, "Sweet Thing, oh Sweet Thing."

She murmured, "Wild Thing, oh Wild Thing."

Wild Thing tasted sweetness. Sweet Thing tasted wildness. They grew very quiet in wonder and awe.

The parents got suspicious at the unusual silence and paid attention. The father investigated and caught them like that, in bed together tasting sweetness and wildness. And the mother whacked Sweet Thing, whacked her even harder than Wild Thing ever got whacked. The passion had mostly gone out of the whacks they gave Wild Thing, as passion does go with things we get used to. But Sweet Thing's loving disobedience was new and much more disturbing than Wild Thing's wildness. She was whacked with a stick that left her bottom bruised. It swelled red and then turned blue by the next morning.

In the meantime, Wild Thing was outdoing himself with roaring. He roared so loudly at having sweetness, so strange and briefly tasted, taken away that he roused the whole countryside, even used as they were to his roaring. The neighbors summoned the law which came thundering in on galloping horses, creating a hellish din throughout the land: alarm bells ringing, Wild Thing roaring, parents whacking, Sweet Thing wailing. It changed things forever.

For when the law finally calmed things down, it was decided that a council must be convened to decide what to do. And so it was that the Council of Wise Men met at some distance from the house so that they could hear one another away from roaring Wild Thing and wailing Sweet Thing. They decreed that Wild Thing and Sweet Thing must be kept very far apart. They considered Wild Thing hopeless and chained him up forever in a dark corner of the cellar near the furnace. The corner was much too hot and dry in winter when the furnace was running and much too cold and damp in the summer. Thus Wild Thing was always in an agony of discomfort, burning or freezing, which fired his rage all the time and kept him roaring all his waking hours. But he was now so far underground that his roar was muffled to a tolerable grumble. He was adequately fed and largely forgotten as we do forget things we get used to.

Wild Thing forgot sweetness and grew wilder and wilder. Sometimes in the wee hours, he whimpered in his sleep, murmuring, "Sweet Thing, oh Sweet Thing." No one heard.

Meanwhile, it was decreed that Sweet Thing, because of her exceeding desire to please, could be redeemed. They locked her up in a tower that could only be reached by a narrow, winding staircase. Her tower room was walled by windows on all sides to allow the maximum amount of light, light being essential, it was thought, for redemption. It was airy and high. She had clouds and birds for company.

In the days following her entowerment, the dark blue of her bruising slowly faded through the pale green and gold of healing. But she couldn't see it. She was busy blocking out the memories and din of transgression.

In that rarefied atmosphere, Sweet Thing grew very good and learned to love everything that could only touch her with the most delicate softness. She talked with birds and clouds. She caressed the light with her voice, singing hymns of praise that floated out over the land, a soprano counterpoint to the bass, subterranean grumble from below. The people of the land rejoiced to hear that counterpoint and gathered together on Sunday morning to sing in harmony and give thanks for Wild Thing's enchainment and Sweet Thing's redemption.

Sweet Thing forgot wildness and grew sweeter and sweeter. She became a saintly visionary, and her dark night-time whimpers were muffled by her pillow and unheard. No one wanted to hear.

Time went on, a long, long time. The parents grew old and died. The Council of Wise Men hired caretakers for Wild Thing and Sweet Thing who did not grow up. They grew wilder and sweeter in their entrapment. The people continued to gather on Sunday mornings to sing in harmony, to rejoice at the powers of enchainment and redemption. But the passion gradually went out of their rejoicing as it does with things we get used to.

One stormy night a beggar from a distant land came up to the door of the big old house where the two were born, long, long ago. She was hungry and cold and tired, and she meant to ask for food and shelter for the night. She meant to, if necessary, as she had times without number, offer her body in exchange. But she saw the door wide open and heard from a distant room the sounds of drunken revelry's final stages. The caretakers were having a party as they did every night to put themselves to sleep.

The beggar walked right through the door and back to the kitchen where she fell to with a hearty appetite, ate her fill and retired on the run in front of the fire. Full and warm and comfortable, she sighed one long sigh and fell into a deep sleep to the party music and a bass grumble below. Wild Thing's rest was being disturbed by the revelers, and he roared.

In the wee hours, the caretakers fell into their drunken sleep. Then it was that the beggar woke with a start and listened in the silence to faint sounds of whimpering above and below. This beggar's heart was soft to the sound of crying. She had lived for centuries, so it seemed, had her heart broken over and over again, and by this long exposure to her own crying in the world, she had grown to hear all cries as her own. As she lay there and listened, her own tears flowed, her chest heaved, her body shuddered, she sobbed aloud.

Just getting down to sleep, Wild Thing, at the sound of this strange sobbing, awoke from his whimper with a roar that would have surely roused the caretakers if they were not so fogged with party spirits. Since they were, they just waved their hands in the air as though waving off a buzzing mosquito and sank back into their stupor. The beggar, though, rose from her rug, lit a candle from the dying embers, and made her way toward Wild Thing's roar which she heard clearly now as a very loud whimper.

Shuddering in the throes of her sympathetic agony, the

beggar found the fearsome Wild Thing straining at his chains and roaring with all his might, his teeth bared, his nostrils flaring, his eyes shooting flames, his horrible horns thrusting at the poor, trembling beggar.

The beggar hesitated a moment only at the appearance Wild Thing presented. She said aloud with a shrug, "I must do something, or I shall never get back to sleep, and what do I have to lose?" She set the candle down, opened her arms, walked right up to Wild Thing, hugged him close, and kissed him right on that fearsome, toothy mouth.

Wild Thing went faint and limp with surprise. He remembered sweetness long, long ago, and he began to sob loudly with grief at the loss. Together they sobbed. Chests heaved. Bodies shuddered. Tears flowed and mingled. Wild Thing and the beggar cried and cried until they were exhausted crying their grief. Then they lay down together, huddling closely for comfort.

There, in the quiet of exhaustion, they heard soft whimpering echoing down the depths from far, far above. Wild Thing moaned and whimpered in response, in the shame and bliss of remembering, "Sweet Thing, oh Sweet Thing." The beggar's eyes overflowed again. Her chest heaved and her body shuddered. Wild Thing kept murmuring.

So the beggar said again, "Ah well, what do I have to lose; I must get some sleep." She took the sputtering candle and went to find a fresh replacement. Getting to Sweet Thing wasn't easy. After trudging up the narrow, winding staircase, she found the tower door locked fast. She had to make her way back down the stairs toward the sound of the caretaker's snoring. As she went, she softly sang a song of praise for some effects of party spirits. With that little bit of created faith, the actual theft was easy. The caretakers had no reason to fear for anyone stealing the keys. No one had ever tried to free Sweet Thing or Wild Thing before. Indeed, all the land was grateful for the way things were, as we get with things we are used to.

In truth, the beggar had no desire to disturb the way things were either. She just wanted to get some sleep which was difficult for her in this particular situation with her quirky trait of feeling everyone's crying as her own. So she stole the keys hanging on the door, locked the caretakers in with their sleep, trudged her way back up the long staircase, and opened the door.

Now Sweet Thing hadn't seen anyone but caretakers since her banishment. She had gotten exceedingly sweet, her sweetness fueled by passions of fear and shame and isolation. And so when she saw the strange beggar, she was in a terror of indecision—on the one hand intense desire to welcome and please her, on the other intense fear of her as a possible whacker. She whimpered and huddled into herself. For the beggar, after Wild Thing, Sweet Thing was a pure delight. She did not hesitate a moment, but set down her candle, opened her arms, took Sweet Thing in a loose, tender embrace, and kissed her softly on her trembling mouth. Tears flowed, chests heaved, bodies shuddered in loud, mingled sobs of grief and remembrance. "Wild Thing, oh Wild Thing," Sweet Thing murmured.

From the cellar echoed, "Sweet Thing, oh Sweet Thing."

The beggar and Sweet Thing made their way down the steep, narrow, winding stairway and thence to the cellar, the beggar holding tightly to the keys.

And so they went through it all again at the reunion of Sweet Thing and Wild Thing. Three now together, huddling: tears flowing, chests heaving, bodies shuddering in the agony and bliss of remembering. They exhausted their grief in that long, long night.

Finally, the beggar remembered the keys and unlocked Wild Thing's chains. *Lo!* Suddenly no one was tired anymore; they were charged with energy. The beggar gathered candles to light their way and they went exploring together through the cellar and house and tower, whooping their joy and singing praises.

And stopping to fight and shout occasionally. Free, Sweet Thing remembered and was mad at Wild Thing for those long ago whacks, and told him so, shouting right in his face. Free, she was feeling wildness. Free, Wild Thing remembered and was jealous that Sweet Thing got smiles for her sweetness when he got only whacks for his wildness, and he drew back his hand to whack her again. But she smiled her sweet smile and reached out her arms.

What could he do? He hugged her. Free, he was feeling

sweetness.

The beggar tagged along, remembering, and sang aloud in empathy with sweetness and wildness, "Forgive." Thus they made their way by the light of the many candles through the cellar and house, looking at everything as if for the first time. And indeed it was first sight, as vision is in freedom. At the threshold of the steep and winding stairs, the beggar gave them the ring of keys and left them. She understood now, she had other work to do in the world.

When Sweet Thing and Wild Thing entered, the sun was rising and flooding the tower room with rosy light streaked by pale green and gold. They remembered they were once one, and they reminisced for hours in hushed tones. At last, as the rose and green of dawn faded to the clear gold of midday, they lay down together and slept. And Lo! Sweet Thing and Wild Thing became Sweet Wild Thing, one and indivisible, a holy union. It changed things forever.

Thus a beggar, in pity and love and faith and hope for peace, freed the world because she had nothing to lose. And because forever only lasts until something changes.

The Miracle

by Patricia Farewell

To sharpen a knife
and cut
     into my own flesh
had never been my goal,
exactly.
     It just sort of
happened. The knife was there:
a gift
     at birth,
I think.
     Often it shone
much better than the water
outside my window,
          water
that was clearly mine
to swim in.
     Sometimes
it promised a kind of
fidelity:
     I will be yours
forever. . .
     But don't get me
wrong. I'm not talking about
deep cuts and blood spurting . . .
Only quick nicks and a
small regular trickle,
         a thin
stream in the woods.
     Yet daily,
I can't deny it.

And for quite a while
I missed the bright boats
in the bay and the clouds—
purple, pink, white and gray—
racing high over the mountains.
                              Still,
to list what I was missing
never saved me.
That took
the miracle:
                    One day I just dropped the knife
and said out loud:
                    It's okay, honey.
                    You can go home now.
                    Your dinner's on the table
                    and it's getting cold.
                    I'm ready to hear
                    whatever you have to say,
                    and if you would rather be silent,
                    that will be fine, too,
                    whatever you want will be fine.

Homecoming

by Kay Marie Porterfield

Once upon a time my brother and I will take the long way back from the cemetery, past the farm where we grew up twenty years ago, the farm my father sold soon after I left home. Paint will peel from the sides of the house, and pale gray curtains flap from shattered windows like ghosts reaching out to grab me. Outbuildings will lean drunkenly. The once neat lawn will be overgrown with tall, ragged grass and unruly bushes. Cornflower, Queen Anne's lace and wild mustard will splash the ditchbanks with color. Even the fields will be filled with blue, white and yellow patches almost obscuring the neat, green rows of soybeans and wheat.

Growing up, we were taught a lesson handed down from generation to generation—that nothing good ever grew naturally from the fertile Michigan soil. No matter how beautiful, whatever sprouted without planning, planting or fertilizing was a weed to be cut, pulled up by the root or poisoned. My father and his ancestors were proper Scots-Irish farmers, who believed in taming their land and their children.

It isn't grief my brother and I will share, as he slows his rented, black T-Bird in front of the three-story Victorian farmhouse, but relief at having survived to adulthood. And pleasure at witnessing the acreage revert to a natural state, the triumph of wildness.

Wild: *Uncultivated, undomesticated, uncivilized, disorderly, messy, disheveled, barbaric, savage.*

Once upon a time running across damp grass in bare feet, I ignored the stars suspended in the night sky, focusing instead on the fireflies always hovering out of reach no matter how fast

I chased them. The trees called my name as I wove intricate patterns across the yard and whooped for joy at the pure, intoxicating pleasure of being six years old on a summer night, gave a cry of thanksgiving for the blood and bone and flesh that were mine, for the fireflies that wouldn't be caught inside the Mason jar I carried.

"Stop running around like a wild woman," my mother called from the back porch. "Come inside this house this instant."

Inside was where my family sat silent around the dinner table and later in the living room. Talking was the same as interrupting, resulting in banishment to my room. Laughing brought exile and a pants-down spanking. Singing, even to myself, merited a pants-down spanking with the razor strop. Singing was for church on Sundays. So I sat mute and unmoving with my knees together as my mother had ordered me to do, listening to the rustle of my father's newspaper, the ticking of the clock. Children were to be seen, not heard. But maybe if I was good enough Dad would take me on his lap behind his fortress of newsprint and read me Alley-Oop.

Wild: *coarse, vulgar, lewd, indecent.*

Once upon a time in the land of earliest memories, my mother calls me into the bathroom. Her face is stamped with grim determination, and I am afraid I have done something wrong again like leaving the faucet to drip or smudging her best wedding-present towels with my handprints. Jerking me by the arm, she pulls me toward the toilet and points a shaking finger at the blood and clots of bloody bathroom tissue in the bowl. "That's what happens to women." Her words are hard as stones. "It's called the curse. Someday you will have the curse. Your body is bad and God will make you bleed for it." She puts her hand on the back of my neck and her cold fingers tighten, pushing my head forward so I will be sure to see.

Is it before this or after it that she begins paying strict attention to my lack of cleanliness? No matter. I cannot recall a time when she has not supervised the daily baths I must take when my father is at work in the fields. She instructs me that if I ever let a man touch me "down there" or do that myself, something bad will happen to me, so bad I will never have babies, or I might bleed to death. "That part of you is evil," she says, "sinful." And then, "The devil made women that way. Before Eve took the apple from the snake, she didn't even have one of those dirty, smelly things." And she scrubs me there with a toothbrush and Fels Naphtha soap until my blood turns the water pink. Only the tropical fish decals languidly floating on the wall above the tub see. They say nothing.

Wild: *crazy, hysterical, out of control.*

Once upon a time I can bear it no longer, and I stand under the old box elder tree between the house and barn, crying and screaming until my lungs burn and my voice goes hoarse. They call it a temper tantrum. My mother commands my father to make me stop. He never, that I can recall, initiates one of these thrashings but strikes me only on my mother's orders. Today when his razor strop whizzes through the air, I scream louder, my wails rising with each lash. The only thing that makes me stop is losing my voice completely. Tears continue to seep from my eyes for three days.

Then it is my mother's turn. She is chronically depressed but not diagnosed or treated, so she spends hours weeping in her room while I stand on a chair to cook my father's dinner and iron his shirts. Work is a good thing, the only thing that will redeem me. If I work hard enough, perhaps I will escape being cursed.

My mother's troubles are all her mother's fault. Grandma was wild when she was a girl, and her brother and sisters are all alcoholics, proof of their shanty Irish ancestry. The only reason Grandma isn't an alcoholic is because she vowed not to touch a drop of the terrible stuff and that lips that touched liquor would never touch hers. Grandpa drinks, but he hides it, except for the cough syrup he always carries with him. Sometimes he lets me have a nip. It tastes like the syrup the druggist puts in cherry Cokes, and it makes me dizzy. Not to be outdone, Grandma occasionally lets me have a taste of the paregoric she must take for her stomach troubles. Even though its bitterness shrivels the inside of my mouth, I keep coming back for one more swallow.

To make Grandma even more dangerous, she was raised a Catholic although she turned away from it later. That's why she plays cards and has parties. That's why she likes the movies, is too sentimental and lets me stay up late when I spend the night with her and Grandpa. Irish Roman Catholics are the closest you can come to pagans. When my mother tells me this, she talks through clenched teeth without moving her lips. They are shameless people, a step away from heathenism.

We are Methodists, she says, and Methodists have the good sense to feel shame and plenty of it. It is the only thing that saves us from burning an eternity in hell, the fat beneath our skin sizzling and popping like bacon in the skillet. Every Sunday when I drink the blood of our dear, precious Jesus, it stains my tongue purple. Suffer the little children washed in the blood of the lamb. World without end. Amen.

Wild: *madcap, rebellious, undisciplined, headlong, unguarded, reckless.*

Once upon a time years later, during the sixties, I will believe I have managed to escape because of my own cleverness. My mind, the only part of me not driven underground, will lead me through the maze of fences and twisted farm lanes of childhood to the state university where I will discover History of Civilization 122 (MWF 9-950, 3 cr hrs) and Comparative Religion 101 (TT 4-450, 2 cr hrs).

There I will learn about Saint Paul, Saint Augustine and other early church fathers who believed that everything natural is evil and must be conquered and domesticated or completely wiped out. This philosophy will sound chillingly familiar. I will find out that my own Scots-Irish ancestors were sent to civilize my savage Irish ancestors during King James' Plantation Movement in the 1600's, the same movement that established the Jamestown colony in this country. I will hear about the witch burnings that killed nine million people, mostly women, in Europe and the convert-or-die mentality responsible for the wholesale slaughter of Native People on this shore, the greed dressed in theology that destroyed the land.

My outrage will be surpassed only by my helplessness against the seemingly unstoppable rape called civilization. First I will cope by growing my hair long, by wearing paisley mini-skirts and peace symbol earrings and by playing Sgt. Pepper's Lonely Hearts Club Band over and over until the album wears out. Then I will trade Sunday services at the campus Wesley Center for SDS meetings held in a ramshackle house reeking of cigarette smoke and mimeograph ink. Every other word out of my mouth will be fuck. Cool and radical as I believe I have become, I will only pretend to smoke pot. It doesn't do much for me, not the way a good, stiff drink helps me unwind.

Wild: *wanton, morally loose, licentious, promiscuous.*

Once upon a time, time after time, Chablis gets me by. The memory of my first drink, two years earlier, is permanently etched in my brain and my biochemistry. I'd visited my aunt and her husband, a lawyer for the Federal Trade Commission. Sitting at the dining table, surrounded by mid-level Kennedy appointees desperate to keep their jobs under the new Johnson regime, I'd thought it only natural to have my wine glass filled, only sophisticated to keep sipping through refill after refill while my skin warmed and my blood sizzled. For the first time in my life since the night of the fireflies, I felt euphoric. While the men droned on about economic policy and the Vietnam War, I savored a private insight—I hadn't found a loving God in church all those years I'd attended, but now, when I least expected it, I'd found Him in a bottle.

For a while I concentrated on pink Chablis, bottle after bubbly, blissful, heart-numbing bottle of it, and then in college on any alcoholic beverage offered me. When I was drunk I could act a little wild, and it seemed that the events of my childhood had happened to someone else.

I ask you, in the era of free love, what's a girl to do when she's terrified of the damning consequences of being touched by a man and is expected to lose her virginity by the end of her freshman year? I'll tell you. She does what works. She learns to drink the blind-date fraternity boys under the table so they always pass out before she does, and just in case, she wears an elastic girdle a size too small. Until she meets Joel.

Tall, thin and exotically Jewish, he wears wire-rimmed glasses, rides a battered Indian motorcycle and writes poetry.

She meets him in a creative writing night class. He ferries her back to her dorm on his bike and then a few weeks later to SDS meetings. She likes to circle his waist with her arms and rub her face against his brown leather bomber jacket when he makes tight turns. He teaches her to smoke French and Turkish cigarettes without filters and to drink espresso. He takes her to movies with subtitles and to dim bars filled with intellectuals and literary types in tight jeans and baggy Irish fishermen's sweaters. Then during midnight walks in the woods, walks that end in beery kisses and an entanglement of arms, he begins reading the poems he writes to her.

Final exam week, when it comes time for her to lose her virginity, he borrows his roommate's car and buys her a bottle of Cutty Sark. They drive to a cow pasture outside of town on the coldest night in winter. This time he sidesteps poetry and kisses, getting right to the point, stripping off the jeans and Irish fisherman's sweater she has taken lately to wearing. When he can't get an erection, he swears. When she doesn't help him because she has no idea of what to do, he swears at her. Finally he climaxes, wet and sticky, a good ten inches from his intended target. Without comment he drives her to the dorm.

Only then does he turn to her. His glasses are fogged over. "You used birth control, I hope." His tone is menacing. "Because if you get knocked up and come crying to me, I'll have all the guys on my floor sign a paper saying you pulled a train."

It will be weeks later before she learns that to pull a train means the same as inciting a gang bang, but already she feels violated, so dirty she takes a scalding shower and fights the urge to scrub her skin with hairbrush and cleanser. Her virginity is intact, yes, but she has lost her innocence, a common theme in contemporary American literature, as her writing professor would say. The betrayal turns her cynical, even though it will be months later when she finds out Joel was engaged to a girl in Detroit during the entire seduction, that the poems he wrote were for his fianceé.

By then it doesn't matter anymore. She's upped her drinking so that the whole, sordid scene in the cow pasture seems to have happened to someone else. By then she is safely married to an engineering student who insists on watching TV until dawn on their wedding night and whose favorite saying is: Love is for ladies; sex is for whores. When she bleeds he sleeps in the living room and insists she dispose of each soiled Kotex immediately in the incinerator down the hall of the married housing building.

Some would say she has come to a sorry state of affairs, but she takes a peculiar comfort in her trips to the incinerator room. They remind her of her mother's Methodist hell. Besides on the rare occasions he makes love, he does so without touching her with his hands, a minor miracle when she thinks of it. As long as she plays the domestic role, typing his papers and making his dinner on time, he encourages her disinterest in sex and doesn't greatly mind that she drinks too much.

Wild: *frenzied, frantic, delirious, berserk.*

Once upon a time that seems timeless, I decide that getting a crescent moon, a Celtic symbol, tattooed on my butt will solve everything wrong with me. So what if I like to drink? I thirst for Spirit and quench that thirst with spirits. That is the legacy of my Irish genes, the same as my way with words. The night after the needle pierces my skin I run naked and clumsy through an abandoned stand of date palms behind my apartment complex, trying to recapture the ecstasy of the firefly night. My body aches as both ground and sky spin in an out-of-kilter dance. The trees aren't talking this time. Not a word.

This is a few years after the divorce, I believe, a divorce I demanded on the grounds that engineers were terminally boring and that this particular one didn't drink enough. He made me look bad, a deliberate anti-feminist move, I concluded after he volunteered to do his mother's taxes, flagrantly cheated and then prayed nightly she'd get caught and sent to jail.

In the tattoo season that is punctuated by occasional blackouts, I am involved again, this time with a man who knows how to have a good time. He turns up the volume on Bob Dylan, fills an old corncob pipe with strong Mexican grass and demands I lie back on the pillows and inhale. Dope will make the sex better, he instructs. He is right. I have my first orgasm. This must be love. At any rate, once I have slept with him, marriage is the only way to avoid the fires of hell. Perhaps he will save me from myself. So I marry him despite our incompatible astrological signs. When I give birth to his child, I remember my mother and the silent fish swimming above the bathtub. Relief floods me.

All things considered, our lives seem to go well except that he hates to work and is always stoned. He expects me to support him while he finds himself. I need to be always intoxicated. This causes a conflict. This and the fact that he suddenly announces he must have more than one woman. How about we try wife swapping or group sex to put a little zip into our relationship? This and the fact that I suspect he uses cocaine and is getting it on with his disco dancing partner.

In self-defense, I enroll our child in daycare and begin passing out by five in the afternoon. If I needed my husband, it would be different, but I don't need him or anyone, just a half-gallon of Ernest & Julio or a couple six-packs of beer and a fifth of Scotch, liquid love. When he leaves me for good, I am too drunk to notice his absence for more than a few days.

Wild: *violent, furious, ravaging, destructive, dangerous.*

Once upon a time in a rare, lucid moment a lover and I will head for Taos on a camping trip. I won't love him and he'll be terrible in bed, but he'll drink the same brand of Scotch as I do and have unlimited credit at the liquor store. Unlike even a year ago, now I won't be able to predict the effects of the alcohol I drink. Sometimes a whole bottle of Scotch will fail to get me high. Other times one beer will propel me, reeling and staggering, into delusions. I won't know whether a drink will send me into a rage or a depression, either of which I will vent shamelessly. I will know that I have to start drinking every morning as soon as the shame does finally hit and I finish throwing up. Without a drink, I will die.

We'll find an appropriate place to set up the tent among the dusty cottonwoods lining the river that winds through Kit Carson Forest. And then we'll head into town for a few Margaritas at the bar in the Taos Inn, stopping at the liquor store on the way back to stock up on camping supplies.

When we arrive at the tent, we'll find a group of six locals drinking wine around the picnic table at our campsite. It will be obvious they've rummaged through our belongings and they have hunting knives. Under the circumstances, we will feel obligated to accept their invitation to drink with them. We'll even try to make the best of a bad situation by bringing our case of beer from the trunk of the car and attempting a joke or two. After one beer I will begin speaking high school Spanish. After two beers I will see the Angel of Death and speak in tongues. From that point on I will sit on the picnic bench, knees together mute and unmoving, waiting to black out, waiting for death to take me.

Two hours later our guests will leave, taking one sleeping bag and the camp stove. We are lucky to be alive, I'll think, but I won't have time to voice my gratitude before my companion will tell me I am a bitch for suggesting this trip and smash his fist into my mouth. All women are bitches, he will tell me. Nasty, evil, arrogant bitches. "I know you wanted those men," he'll accuse. "I know you're disappointed nobody raped you, you no-good whore." My front teeth will come loose and I will taste blood.

When he begins working on my eyes, I will think I see fireflies, but before I can run, he'll rip my tee shirt and swing at my breasts with a felled tree branch, leaving scars that will persist for years. I'll try to escape into the tent which he will tear to shreds, and then he'll jerk me by the arm to the creek, smashing my face against the stones beneath the water. When I try to fight back, he will pin my arms behind me with one hand. Then he will pull out my hair with his other hand. Although I will scream and scream until my lungs burn, no one will come to my rescue.

"I want to kill you, bitch," he will say before he drives away leaving me to die. "But that would be too good for you, too damned good." And only when I hear the roar of his engine climbing the hill, the squeal of tires against pavement, will I wrap the torn, blue scraps of tent around me and allow myself the luxury of unconsciousness.

Sober: *not intoxicated, joyless, severe, restrained, somber, drab, chaste, unimaginative.*

Once upon a time the man who called himself my lover experienced a change of heart and returned to rescue me. He immediately deposited me in a cheap Santa Fe motel room, swore me to secrecy about what he'd done, and to emphasize the seriousness of the vow, beat me again. When our money ran out, we returned to Phoenix despite my black eyes and bruised, lacerated flesh.

There we began drinking even more than before, trying to blot out the incident. While I licked my wounds, he stalked my apartment ready to attack again at the first opening he could find. Within days I knew I had to do something; it was a matter of life and death. Pouring an iced-tea tumbler full of warm Scotch and gulping half of it, I dialed the number of a battered women's shelter.

"What your boyfriend did is wrong," the counselor told me during our first appointment—after she had asked me how much I drank, and I lied to her in order to protect what I considered a basic necessity of life, more important than food or shelter. "What you're doing to yourself is wrong, too," she continued. You're drinking yourself to death. Keep going and your liver will give out or you'll commit suicide or be killed. You're an alcoholic, and you need to sober up."

Immediately I argued with her. "Who, me? I couldn't be. I'm too clever and talented to be an alcoholic. I have a college degree." But a sense of relief began to seep insidiously through the hairline cracks in my alcoholic denial, relief I couldn't keep myself from feeling. If I had a disease, a legitimate disease, then maybe I wasn't crazy as I'd believed for most of my life.

Treatment for what was wrong with me was as easy as stopping drinking and attending A.A. meetings, the counselor advised. Even then the simplicity of her method had a hollow ring to it, but I knew an untimely death would await me if I continued my enslavement to alcohol. Since I needed to take some sort of action and her plan was the only one forthcoming, I decided to give it a try.

Dragging myself home, I collapsed on the unmade bed and scattered pamphlets about alcoholism across the rumpled sheets, but my hands shook so hard I couldn't read them. Instead I turned on the TV and stared vacantly as Wiley Coyote tried to outsmart Roadrunner. In the meantime my body alternated between cold and hot sweats until the reek of metabolized booze leaking through my pores offended even me.

My head pounded and my stomach heaved. When I managed to doze off, nightmares tormented me. Asleep or awake, every cell shrieked out for my daemon lover, alcohol.

After two days of this, I crept into the back row of my first A.A. meeting at a run-down rehab center a few blocks from where I lived. From the backslapping to the slogans, the structure of the meeting reminded me of the evangelical churches of my childhood. The speaker even gave a drunkalog, a lengthy tale of his descent into the hellish pit of alcoholism and his salvation from depravity through A.A., reminiscent of the endless Christian testimonials I'd heard as a child. Although addiction was officially labeled disease rather than wickedness, evil was heavily implied, and I felt overwhelmed by shame for what I'd done, for who I was inside. Convicted of my original sin, I needed a drink more than ever. But I kept coming back, and eventually abstaining became easier. A.A. worked just as the members intoned at the conclusion of their meetings. And who was I, an alcoholic sinner, to question what worked? I was sober.

For five years I battled to tame the wild thing inside of me which craved the seductive temptation of alcohol and the ecstatic release it brought, just as frantically as I had wrestled in childhood with the pieces of myself which had offended my mother. I struggled to fit myself as best I could into the many meanings that one word, sober, holds. Turning my back on intoxication in all forms, I practiced restraint. My life became totally focused on avoiding what I could not do. I became harshly strict with myself, as self-mortifying and humorless as any Puritan shunning pagan dangers lurking in the dark woods beyond the settlement. With the dedication my father had practiced at ripping the weeds from his well-tilled fields, I yanked joy, silliness, and pleasure from my life by their roots. Serious, solemn, toned-down, dull and logical, I was sober—stone cold sober. Until I could bear it no longer and again invited the Angel of Death into my life, this time by swallowing a deliberate overdose of painkillers.

Wild: *natural, passionate, untamed, unrestrained, unshackled, unrestricted, unbroken, mighty, strong.*

Sixteen years later I am still coming to. This awakening to

consciousness is not a once upon a time thing. Rather my healing stretches out ahead of me for the duration of this lifetime and perhaps into the next. Neither is my journeying to wholeness continuous. Instead it goes by fits and starts. But I am coming full circle, back to the trees and the weeds, I now know as wildflowers, which sustained me as a child.

Ironically, my botched act of suicidal desperation gave me back the life which had been stolen from me in early childhood, by leading me to a therapist who helped me work through the soul-crushing emotional pain which had impelled me to drink in the first place. This wise woman told me I didn't need to be sober to lead an alcohol-free life. I could choose to be intoxicated with the natural world around me, choose to respect and to affirm the strong, unbroken parts of myself which I had kept hidden for years. Abstaining from alcohol and embracing my inner wildness were not mutually exclusive. She gave me permission to dance with the fireflies, delighting in their freedom and my own.

Over the past ten years, I have learned to trust the healing wisdom my own womanheart holds as well as the keen power of my senses. To talk to the trees again and this time to listen to the sacred truths they speak, to catch the scent of wisdom from the stream rushing through narrow, mossy banks is not madness, but an ancestral form of sanity at the deepest level. I hear and am tutored by the songs of Celtic wildness pulsing through my blood and, although I quaver at times, I am beginning to live out those impassioned prayer songs in a world grown sick and weary with civilization.

The more the Creator and Creation teach me, the more convinced I become that alcoholism is not a disease, but a symptom—Western civilization is the disease which has spread mercilessly from continent to continent, from heart to heart, feeding on the natural, uncontent until it is completely consumed. My savage Irish forebears, although they drank, were not immobilized by alcoholism until forced to give up the Old Religion for Christianity and torn from their land and their language. What first appeared as temporary escape from the harsh emptiness of an oppressed life turned out to be the chains the oppressor used to bind and subdue us. My Native American friends assure me it was the same for their people, who did not even know the synthetic intoxication of alcohol until the trappers, traders and missionaries arrived to civilize them, a synonym for stealing them blind.

I am certain that A.A. helps many people to stop drinking as it did me. I am also certain that for many of us, the brand of sobriety the group offers is not the ultimate answer to the problem of addiction. Evolved from the Oxford Society, a self-improvement group for white male Christians, A.A. attempts to civilize savage alcoholics. For women and people of color and those who identify with their pre-Christian roots, this process only continues the wave of oppression and domination which we have endured for centuries.

Once I fully understood that I did not have to fiercely fight myself to keep from drinking and that an alcohol-free life was the unfettered way I was born to live, I could allow myself to revert to a relatively uncultivated state. In midlife I have become a heathen, one who has returned to the heath, the countryside outside the city walls that mark the boundaries of Christian civilization. Slowly my tribe, my clan, gathers around me. They are too busy honoring the life the Creator has given us to mind that my paint is peeling down to bare wood or that my fields, once planted with straight rows of assumptions and warnings about original sin, have gone to cornflowers and Queen Anne's lace. My recovery has been a journey home in the truest meaning of the word, a celebration of the blood and flesh and bone that are mine and which I share with my partner, a celebration of Spirit. I take pleasure at witnessing this triumph of nature—my nature.

Procedure for Reclaiming the Self

by Patricia Monaghan

she presses eyes and
remembers sight and

touches temples and
remembers blood and

twists her hair and
recalls that

thought
is space

in the hands of a lover she
forgets herself yes

I forget myself
I had forgotten

the outlines of this solitude
this body etched on air

once and transitory, more
lasting than leaves, more

temporary than trees, fleet
compared to stones

now remembering its
edges, its dissolutions

I come back
I always must

come back
this distance

far from you
far into

my wildness
my own oceans

my glacial
splendors

my mountain
silences

my vast
interior plains

About the Authors

Lynn Alldrin's first published poem, "Old Apple Trees," was written for her son, dead at twenty after an alcohol-related accident. "Rude Awakening" alludes to other kinds of loss. She shares, "Grief will always temper my writing, but no longer owns it (thank the Goddess)."

Judith Barrington is the author of two collections of poetry: *Trying to Be an Honest Woman* and *History and Geography*, both published by Eighth Mountain Press. She edited *An Intimate Wilderness: Lesbian Writers on Sexuality*. Her work has appeared recently in The *Women's Review of Books, Kenyon Review* and *Thirteenth Moon*. She recently received a grant from the Oregon Institute of Literary Arts for the collection of Spanish Essays which includes "Sleeping Around."

Gwendolyn Bikis is a Capricorn with Scorpio Rising. She teaches, dances and spends time with the ocean. Her 1993 resolution is to learn to play her saxophone. Portions of the novel from which "Reefer Sadness" was excerpted have been published in *The Persistent Desire, Conditions, Common Lives, Lesbian Lives,* and *Catalyst*. A chapter is forthcoming in *Sister/Stranger* as well.

Sallie Bingham's sixth book, a novel called *Upstate*, will be published by Permanent Press in June of 1993. She is a teacher, poet, playwright and publisher of *The American Voice*, a feminist literary quarterly, and founder of the Kentucky Foundation for Women. She writes from Santa Fe, "The pain of addiction brings all of us together, especially women who have faced loving a man who cannot face his addiction."

Alice Bolstridge is a fiction writer and poet who has been published in *Cimarron Review, Cincinnati Poetry Review, Art Times* and elsewhere. "Sweet Thing and Wild Thing" is one of several tales in her novel, *Story Teller*. She is an adult child in an addictive family system and says that this story, drafted in two days, felt like a gift in a particularly dynamic phase of her recovery. "During this time I became conscious of the healing and integrative power of my writing," she notes. "In writing, I break the power of the no-talk rule that keeps us divided within ourselves and emotionally disconnected from others."

Madelyn Camrud is the 1992 winner of the Minnesota Voices Project Competition for her poetry collection, *This House is Filled With Cracks,* which was published by New Rivers Press. She was raised on a farm near Grand Forks and has lived in North Dakota all of her life. "About fifteen years ago, someone told me to 'write it down.' I've been writing it down ever since, and the writing often evolves into a poem," she says about her work. "Poems allow me to look up, down and crosswise at life. I don't just *like* writing poems; I *need* to write poems."

Melissa Cannon lives in Nashville where she works in the fast food industry. She feels there are positive and negative aspects to a relationship with Dionysus. She writes, "I'd be less inclined to 'just say no' than to agree with William Blake that, 'The road to excess leads to the palace of wisdom.' "

Marilyn Elain Carmen is widely published in the U.S. and Canada in journals such as *Heresies, Black American Literature Forum* and *Sing Heavenly Muse.* She is a recipient of a 1990 Pennsylvania State Arts Grant based on her book, *Blood at the Root,* and is a finalist for residency at California's Headlands Center for the Arts.

Joan Connor's work has been published in *The Northern New England Review, The Kennebec Review* and several anthologies. She is a graduate of Mount Holyoke College and Middlebury's Breadloaf School of English. She divides her time between Essex, Connecticut, and Chebeaque Island, Maine — and the demands of her son Kerry, and her keyboard.

Annie Dawid's first novel, *York Ferry,* was published by Cane Hill Press of NY. One of the sections appeared in *Women on*

Women II. Her fiction has also appeared in *American Fiction 93.* Many of her works deal with substance abuse.

Deborah DeNicola received an MFA in Poetry from the Vermont College Writing Program. She is the winner of the 1992 Embers Chapbook Poetry Competition. Her work has appeared in *Review, The North American Review, Fiction International* and a number of other publications. She has owned and operated a bookstore, been a freelance arts reviewer, worked as a Poet-In-The-Schools and taught at the University of Southern Maine. Currently she is a visiting Lecturer at the Massachusetts College of Art.

Patricia Farewell, whose poems have been published in *The American Poetry Review, The New York Quarterly, The Partisan Review* and *The Little Magazine,* is currently ghostwriting a book about the Inner Voice. Her first book-length manuscript of poetry was a finalist in the Yale Series of Younger Poets competition. A recovering alcoholic, Patricia believes that her participation in a women's group has helped her heal and grow in many unanticipated and exciting ways. Yoga, meditation, keeping a journal, running and swimming are other important tools in her recovery program.

Catherine Gammon has published a novel, *Isabel out of the Rain* (Mercury House, 1991), as well as short fiction in a variety of literary magazines. She has held fellowships from the National Endowment for the Arts, the New York Foundation for the Arts, and the Fine Arts Work Center in Provincetown. After ten years in New York City, she recently moved to Pittsburgh, where she teaches fiction writing at the University of Pittsburgh.

Pamela Gray, a Jewish lesbian living in Santa Monica, has flirted with and succumbed to various addictions, but now enjoys life in recovery. She is a poet, playwright, and screenwriter whose work appears in many anthologies and journals, including *New Lesbian Writing, Cats and their Dykes* and *Dykescapes.*

JoAnn Bren Guernsey is the author of three young adult novels published by Clarion Books/Houghton Mifflin, two of which deal extensively with sexuality as it colors the adolescent years. She's also had ten nonfiction books published for teen readers dealing with such contemporary issues as teen pregnancy, rape and abortion. She's now at work on a book on sexual harassment.

Anne Stirling Hastings, Ph.D. is a psychologist in Bellevue, Washington, where she specializes in sexuality. A recovering sex addict and incest survivor, she wrote *Reclaiming Healthy Sexual Energy* (Health Communications, Inc., 1991). Her next two books, *The Second Sexual Revolution* and *Crosswired: Learning About Adults Who are Sexual With Children,* will be available in early 1994. In addition to writing and her therapy practice, Anne trains other therapists to work with sexual issues.

Patricia Heyne was born n 1957 in Des Moines, Iowa. She is currently a student of nursing at Front Range Community College in Denver. She is a counselor at a women's shelter and a freelance writer.

Andrea King Kelly is currently in the Ph.D. creative writing program at Florida State University, where she received the 1991 Academy of American Poets Award and a 1991-1992 Kingsbury Writing Fellowship, which was renewed for 1992-1993. She is a member of the board of directors for Anhinga Press and *IQ: International Quarterly*, a new journal of writing, art ideas and culture from around the world.

Zoe Keithley, a native Chicagoan, is a poet and fiction writer. She teaches at Northeastern Illinois University College of Education Chicago Teachers' Center, working with teachers who want to improve their teaching of writing skills in Chicago Public Schools. She also teaches at Columbia College and DePaul University. She is a founding member of the poetry ensemble World Enough and Time and the director of the SOLO! reading series. She says, "After the hard shell cracked, a small, new self wriggled out, and I could thank the disasters. When you sleep with Dionysus, you wake up with a different life."

Paula Legendre is the pseudonym of a woman who graduated with honors in Mechanical Engineering from the University of Colorado in 1977. Now a technical writer, she lives in Boulder with her two children. Her literary work has been published in *Meditations for the Divorced, What's a Nice Girl Like You Doing in a Relationship Like This, Cricket, Single Parent, The Boulder Parent, Cokefish, Just Between Us, Mobius, Pegasus, Skylark* and *Tangents.*

Alison Luterman was born in 1958. Now she lives in Oakland with her husband where she writes, teaches and is learning to sing.

Marnie Maguire is from Ontario, Canada, where she is completing her novel, *Carcass.* She is grateful to Karyn McKnight, whose poetry influenced the making of "Blue."

Rita Markley was graduated summa cum laude from the University of Maryland in 1983. She has been writing short stories and essays for many years and is currently working on her first novel. Her work has been published in the *Dithyrambic Ephemeris and Waste Age.* She is a recovering alcoholic and celebrated her fifth year of sobriety on November 26, 1992. She resides in Burlington, VT.

Lisa Martinovic is a poet, writer and artist from San Francisco who began healing from the spectrum of substance and process addictions in 1982. In 1988 she became the publisher of San Francisco's *Recovering* magazine. She left that job in the interest of deeper healing and in the process blossomed her talents as a poet and visual artist. She also began designing custom jewelry and started a desktop publishing business. Lisa has just released her first book, *Adventures in Coming Alive,* a collection of poetry and color reproductions of her art. She is now at work on a nonfiction book about healing from the way we work in America.

Patricia Monaghan was raised in Alaska, a state of magnificent scenery and the highest rate of alcoholism in the nation. Her family on both sides is Irish-American; thus, she has deep ties to two subcultures in which addiction is prevalent. She is the author of two books of poetry, *Winterburning* (Fireweed Press, 1990) and *Seasons of the Witch* (Delphi Press, 1992) as well as of a nonfiction book, *The Book of Goddesses and Heroines* (E.P. Dutton, 1981; Llewellyn, 1990). Monaghan has also edited three anthologies: *Hunger and Dreams: The Alaskan Women's Anthology, Unlacing: Ten Irish-American Women Poets,* and *Hard Gifts: An Irish-American Anthology.* She is currently at work on a book about dream interpretation, an autobiography of the Blessed Virgin Mary and *Home Deaths,* a collection of poems about families, addiction and war.

Valerie McMillan, who has a Master of Arts in Counseling Psychology, graduated from the University of Denver in 1984. A recovering high school counselor, she has a private practice and specializes in adolescent and sexually abused adult clients. She served for six years on the Human Development Steering Committee for the National League of Cities.

Julie Novak-McSweeney has been a recovering alcoholic since 1983. To her recovery, and to a Power greater than herself, she gratefully credits the reemergence of her creative abilities. A former broadcasting engineer and freelance copy editor, she is a published poet and award-winning playwright. Julie currently lives in California with her alto saxophonist husband, Brian, and two cats.

Hillary Mullins is a thirty-year old dyke recently transplanted from Vermont to Oakland, California, where she lives with her partner and three cats. "The Bear" was born in a moment of vision while she was house-sitting in the Green Mountains. She says, "I wanted to write something that would convey the terror many of us carry and how our power lies waiting just beyond it, waiting for us to seize hold of her. My own abuse of alcohol stemmed in large part from a history of sexual abuse, and the Bear has been a powerful force in my recovery from both." Her first novel, *The Cat Came Back,* which deals with teacher-student sexual abuse and coming out, is being published by Naiad Press in October of 1993.

Norah Philbin comes from a strong family of five daughters and is now the single mother of a ten-year-old son. She says, "Writing is my way to come out of the madness with good form."

Kay Marie Porterfield lives and write in Denver. In her fifteenth year of recovery from alcoholism, she is the author of many books on healing from addiction and domestic violence, including *What's a Nice Girl Like You Doing in a Relationship Like This?* Her most recent book is *Blind Faith: Recognizing and Recovering from Dysfunctional Religious Groups* (CompCare 1993).

Elspeth Cameron Ritchie was born in San Francisco, grew up in Washington, DC, and has lived in Cyprus, Lebanon, Malaysia, Egypt and Korea. Now she resides in Silver Spring, MD, where she tends her rose garden, pumpkin patch and three cats. She is a psychiatrist and a major in the United States Army. Her writing has grown out of an attempt to understand and make coherent both her own life and those of her patients.

Judith Roche's second book, *Myrrh,* appeared in the spring of 1993 from Black Heron Press. She lives in Seattle and is literary arts director of Bumbershoot, Seattle's city arts festival. She teaches through Washington State University's Artist-in-Residence Program.

Cindy Rosmus has had stories in *The North American Review, Out, The Village Idiot, The Unmentionable* and *Thin Ice.* Many are set in a brutal, alcoholic world. About this, she says, "It's a trap, sure, but some women enjoy it. There's a way out, but only if you want it." Cindy is a true "Jersey Girl." She's recently completed a novel of the same name.

Gianna Russo's poems have been published or are forthcoming in *Poet Lore, Calyx, South Florida Poetry Review, New Collage, Palmetto Review, Organica, The Tampa Tribune, Fiction Quarterly* and others. She was a winner in the 1990 Hillsborough County Arts Council Statewide Poetry Competition. She has designed and conducts fiction and poetry workshops for the Tampa Museum of Art. She teaches creative writing at the University of South Florida and is a managing editor for the Tampa Bay Review.

Mary Ann Schaefer is a 36-year-old Colorado transplant who recently celebrated six years of sobriety. She has a BA in journalism from the University of Nebraska and currently works as a freelance writer and poet. She lives in the mountains with her odd-eyed dog, Karma, and her long-time companion, a 15-year-old cat named Toby.

Jennifer Semple Siegel teaches part-time at York College of Pennsylvania and is a tutor at the writing center. Her work has been published in *Yugoslav English Language Teaching Review, Eating Our Hearts Out: Women and Food* and *The Dictionary of Literary Biography*.

Ruth Shaer is a poet, storyteller and essayist, as well as a feature and business writer. Her poetry is forthcoming in *Women Dancing Free,* an anthology by women who have broken free of oppressive situations. Her fiction has been published in *Athena*. Born in London, she immigrated to the United States in 1981 and lives in Los Angeles with her husband. Of her work, she comments, "My writing is rooted in a quest for authenticity, connecting with the Higher Self and breaking free from negative and illusionary influences."

Jackie Sheeler has been writing for over twenty years, but has only recently made serious efforts toward publication. Her poems and essays have appeared in *Encore, Contact II, The New York Press* and an anthology, *New Voices*. She writes, "As a recovering addict, I find writing to be a valuable tool in learning to recognize and deal with feelings, situations and events and in forming new responses to the world around me. When I "run" today, I'm running for the pen and paper to try and create something magical (a poem, a story, a song) rather than trying to destroy something magical (a person, a lifetime, a home).

Cameron Sperry recently completed her MA in creative writing at the University of North Carolina in Wilmington, where she is employed as a lecturer in the English Department. She has also worked as a journalist and a writing consultant. "Steps" is her first published short story. She lives in Wrightsville Beach, North Carolina, with her husband, George.

Sheryl St. Germain teaches creative writing and literature at The University of Southwestern Louisiana. Her work has received many awards, including an NEA Fellowship, the Dobie-Paisano Fellowship and the Ki Davis Award from the Aspen Writers Foundation. Her books include *Going Home* (Perivale Press, 1989) and *The Mask of Medusa* (Cross Cultural, 1987). Her most recent book is *Making Bread at Midnight* (Slough Press, 1992), which was published with a grant from the Texas Council on the Arts. She writes from Lafayette, Louisiana, where she lives with her son, "I have an unusual relationship with addiction, in that both my brother and my father, two people I loved very deeply, died as a result of their chemical addictions. I have shared both of their addictions, and part of my desire to write has to do with wanting to articulate with compassion and without judgment, the complexity of the nature of obsession and addiction. Being able to write the 'truth' of addiction has allowed me to do more than survive; it has allowed me to move to a level of insight and compassion that would have otherwise been impossible."

Alison Stone's poems have appeared in *Poetry, The Paris Review, Ploughshares, New York Quarterly, Catholic Girls* and a variety of other magazines and anthologies. She is also a painter, a Witch and a Reiki healer. Her first book, *What the Body Knows,* is currently seeking a publisher.

Celia Stuart-Powels writes poetry under the pseudonyms Morning Star and Celestia. Her major area of study was visual art, and she makes her "living" as an electrical designer. She also serves as a council member for Circles of Exchange, a women's correspondence network, exploring the many faces of the Goddess.

Michelle M. Tokarczyk was born and raised in a working-class family in New York City. She received her BA from Herbert Lehman College and, after a couple of false starts, began and completed the Ph.D. program in English at SUNY Stony Brook. In 1989, she broke her dependence with New York City and accepted an appointment with Goucher College. Her books include a collection of poetry, *The House I'm Running From*. In addition to balancing the demands of teaching and writing, Michelle juggles a commuter marriage with a spouse still in the Big Apple.

Cheryl Townsend edits *Impetus*, a literary magazine, from Stowe, Ohio. Her poetry has appeared in *Amelia, Feminist Voices, Pearl* and a number of other publications. She has four chapbooks available from various small presses.

Devon Vose is a poet writing near Seattle. She received a BA in Literature from Humboldt State University. Her poems have appeared in *Bellowing Ark, Hecate's Loom, Journey, Lynx, Sacred River* and other publications.

Anne F. Walker was born in Berkeley, California and moved to Toronto when she was seven. This affected her deeply and was when she began to write. Since 1984 she has published in a number of magazines and anthologies, received arts grants and co-wrote a feature film as well as a documentary. Her two collections of poetry are *Six Months Rent* and *Pregnant Poems*. Her sweetheart, son and she divide their time between Oakland and Toronto.

Jean Walton Wolf was born in northern California. She was raised there and in Latin America by an alcoholic mother who eventually took her own life. For Jean writing is a tool for healing, as well as for bringing beauty into the world. She believes, "Women like us who have been touched by alcoholism often have a deep compassion and gratitude for life. The scourge becomes the blessing." The story, "Night Bridges," was inspired while driving to Esalen to attend a writing workshop. Her work has appeared in several literary magazines, and she facilitates retreats and creative writing workshops for women in recovery and others.

Lisa Horton Zimmerman received her MFA from Washington University in St. Louis in 1983. She lives with her husband and their three children in Fort Collins, Colorado. She writes, "I come from a family with a history of alcoholism. My fiction often speaks to that pain and separation and with hope."

Marti ZuckroV says she is a 48 year old woman who has been lucky to find creativity so that she can stay sane, create art, heal and have fun. She's danced and choreographed since she was a child. For five years she was artistic director and choreographer for Dancespace, a women's dance company in Berkeley. Currently she is working on a short novel about growing up as a Red Diaper Baby.

The Crossing Press
publishes a full selection of titles
of general interest.
To receive our current catalog,
please call, toll free

800-777-1048